PRAISE FOR INSIDE THE SECOND WAVE OF FEMINISM

"An invaluable contribution to the canon of works on the history of the feminist movement in the United States. Nancy Rosenstock has written an absorbing account of what it felt like to be a woman in the America of the '50s and '60s, the awakening of so many of us to the systematic discrimination we faced, and how we fought and overcame it." —**DR. BARBARA ROBERTS**, cofounder of the Women's National Abortion Action Coalition

"Often, the intimately intertwined histories of socialism, anarchism, and gay and women's liberation in America are willfully obscured. Often, second-wave feminists' commitment to overthrowing capitalism is erased, as is their sisterhood with transgender women. Often, the shortcomings and defeats of lesbian separatist organizing are memorialized to the exclusion of the imaginatively rich, experientially complex, frequently surprising archives of 'womyn'-centered struggle we need and deserve to hear about. These are some of the reasons why Nancy Rosenstock's account of the militant collective thought and action of trans-inclusive Bostonian 'females' fifty years ago is an important resource for anyone invested in today's movements for gender liberation and reproductive justice. This is a book dense with vital records of struggles for abortion and child care, struggles lost and won, inspirational testimonies, thoughtful self-appraisals and thrilling documentary artifacts." —**SOPHIE LEWIS**, author of *Full Surrogacy Now* and *Abolish the Family*

"Not only is this book a fi.......................................ly implistic and whitewashed po...........................m, but it

T0150880

also honors the scrappy, homegrown, grassroots radical feminist histories of Boston's Cell 16. Nancy Rosenstock provides a beautiful window into the nuances of starting a movement, from grunt work, growing armpit hair, and marching in the streets to lesbian separatism, tae kwon do classes, and radical abortion rights activism. This account is both historic and fresh, showing us once again that history is alive, written and rewritten by each subsequent cohort of rabble-rousing feminists looking to smash norms and change the world." —**BREANNE FAHS**, editor of *Burn It Down! Feminist Manifestos for the Revolution*

"When Kathie Sarachild of Redstockings coined the phrase 'Sisterhood is Powerful' in 1968, this is what she meant: ordinary women becoming revolutionaries because they had each other—to argue with, build unity with, and risk everything with as they opened new fronts in the fight against male supremacy." —**JENNY BROWN**, author of *Birth Strike* and *Without Apology*.

"A wonderful accounting of the ideas and actions of a singular group of radical feminists, which is enriched by the inclusion of the very documents shaping these individuals and this movement. As one participant said of the group, 'Women were so hungry for this information. It was like being swept up by a wave.' Rosenstock gives an insider's view of the group and its popular journal, *No More Fun and Games*. Just as the group and its journal informed and enriched women's lives and gave them an understanding of the ideals of the Female Liberation group, so too does this book, with its interviews and documents, transport the reader to the historical moment." —**DR. KATHERINE PARKIN**, professor of history at Monmouth University

INSIDE THE SECOND WAVE OF FEMINISM

Boston Female Liberation, 1968–1972
An Account by Participants

Nancy Rosenstock

Haymarket Books
Chicago, Illinois

Published in 2022 by
Haymarket Books
P.O. Box 180165
Chicago, IL 60618
773-583-7884
www.haymarketbooks.org
info@haymarketbooks.org

ISBN: 978-1-64259-704-2

Distributed to the trade in the US through Consortium Book Sales
and Distribution (www.cbsd.com) and internationally through
Ingram Publisher Services International (www.ingramcontent.com).

This book was published with the generous support of Lannan
Foundation and Wallace Action Fund.

Special discounts are available for bulk purchases by organizations
and institutions. Please email info@haymarketbooks.org for more
information.

Cover photography taken at the Women's Strike for Equality,
August 26, 1970, in New York City by Howard Petrick.
Cover design by Rachel Cohen.

Printed in Canada by union labor.

Library of Congress Cataloging-in-Publication data is available.

10 9 8 7 6 5 4 3 2 1

CONTENTS

INTRODUCTION

A little more than a hundred years ago in the United States, women won the right to vote after a long fight.[*] This struggle, often referred to as the "first wave" of feminism, was followed, fifty years later, by what has become known as feminism's "second wave."

What was the second wave of feminism? What did it look like from the inside? Why is it relevant today?

Through interviews with thirteen activists including myself, and through documents spanning the years 1968–1972, this book takes a look at these questions by focusing on one of the major radical feminist groups that developed in the early days of feminism's second wave.

Boston Female Liberation—which for a time was also known as Cell 16—published one of the first feminist journals, *No More Fun and Games*, beginning in 1968. Later, in 1971, we launched a magazine, the *Second Wave*. Both publications were widely read and respected at the time and included poetry, art,

---

[*]   The Nineteenth Amendment to the US Constitution, ratified in 1920, stated that the right to vote would not be denied on account of sex. However, Black women were disenfranchised by Jim Crow laws in the South for decades.

and theoretical articles analyzing female oppression.

Through these publications and its activities, Female Liberation/Cell 16* became a pole of attraction nationally. In 1969 it helped organize the New England Regional Female Liberation Conference, which was attended by over six hundred people. Leaders of Female Liberation were invited to speak at several national women's liberation conferences. One of the main contributions the organization made was to question prevailing notions of "beauty" and "femininity." The organization also became known for teaching self-defense to women to combat sexual violence.

Understanding that women needed to control their own bodies at a time when abortion was illegal, Female Liberation joined others in the fight for the legalization of abortion. In addition, the organization championed the call for "No forced sterilization," knowing that Black, Latina, and Native American women were often sterilized against their will. Working in a coalition with others, Female Liberation led the campaign to place a referendum on the Cambridge, Massachusetts, ballot in 1971 calling for free, twenty-four-hour child care; the referendum won, but the measure was never implemented. Female Liberation was also one of the first radical feminist groups to seek alliances with the anti–Vietnam War movement and the fight for Black liberation. Many of its members became convinced of the ties between feminism and socialism.

Included in the book is a first-hand account of the fifty-thousand-strong, August 26, 1970, march in New York City that heralded the public emergence of the second wave of feminism. Ruthann Miller, official coordinator of the march, though not a

---

*   Throughout the book, the names Boston Female Liberation and Female Liberation are used interchangeably.

member of Boston Female Liberation, was interviewed for this book. She describes the events leading up to the demonstration, as well as on the day of that historic event.*

The book is divided into two parts. The first section is weaved together as a conversation, outlining the path of each woman and of the organization as a whole. Documents of Female Liberation make up the second part. Included here are important contributions to radical feminist theory and practice: "Abortion: A Feminist Perspective," "Why Is Feminism Revolutionary?," "Females and Self-Defense," and "Black Women and Abortion," plus more.

Readers of this book, young and old, will find themselves identifying with the thirteen women interviewed—ordinary women caught up in extraordinary times. Each woman tells her story: growing up in the 1950s, her involvement in radical feminist politics, and her continued belief and activity in defense of women's rights today. The joy and excitement of discovering that one is not alone and then organizing collectively is apparent throughout the pages of this book.

Being part of the women's liberation movement during these momentous years forever changed our lives, as it did for millions of women. Understanding our history and learning from it—both the successes and failures—is vital in confronting the challenges of today.

---

* A longer interview I did with Miller can be found in *Jacobin*, printed in the fall of 2020: Ruthann Miller, "How the Strike for Equality Relaunched the Struggle for Women's Liberation in the US," *Jacobin*, November 1, 2020, https://jacobinmag.com/2020/11/womens-strike-equality-liberation-betty-friedan.

≈

In order to fully grasp the accomplishments of the second wave of feminism, it helps to examine the situation that women faced in the 1960s in the United States. It was one of restricted opportunities on all fronts.

Women seeking employment outside the home found separate job listings for men and women. In 1963, the Commission on the Status of Women released a report revealing that women earned 59 cents for every dollar that men earned. Black women made roughly 40 percent of what white men made. In 1970 only 43 percent of women participated in the workforce, to a large extent in occupations of service, such as secretarial work, teaching, waiting tables, and nursing. Five times as many Black women worked as maids and household cleaners compared to white women in 1972. When employed, restrictions on clothing were common—women in offices were expected to wear a dress or skirt with nylons, not pants. Opportunities for career advancement were limited. Avenues were not open for most women who wanted to be architects, engineers, welders, plumbers, carpenters, or other jobs that were considered at the time to be jobs only for men.

Women lacked full control over their bodies. Abortion was illegal. In fact, according to Planned Parenthood, in 1965, illegal abortions made up one-sixth of all pregnancy- and childbirth-related deaths. Upwards of five thousand women died each year as a result of illegal or self-induced abortions, according to a report put out in 2014 by the American College of Obstetricians and Gynecologists. The mortality rate for nonwhite women was twelve times that for white women. Contraception was difficult to obtain. Women could be fired from their jobs just for being pregnant.

Sexual harassment in the workplace was barely recognized. Domestic violence was a real part of many women's lives, and fighting it was not an easy option. Rape was often not reported because doing so subjected a woman to further harassment and humiliation from the police, and often from her male abuser.

At colleges and universities, female students faced numerous restrictions. Women were channeled into "female occupations," and many were denied the opportunities to pursue studies of their choice—for example, medicine and science. University students faced dress codes and curfews in college dormitories.

One of the most common demeaning experiences women faced during this time was the fact that they were identified almost exclusively by their marital status. You were either a "Miss" or a "Mrs." In fact, if you were married you were often referred to both as "Mrs." and your husband's first and last name. Your identity was completely washed away.

The barriers that women faced economically, increasing their dependency on men, can be seen by the fact that when applying for credit, women were often asked a barrage of questions: Are you married? Do you plan on having children? Many banks required single, divorced, or widowed women to bring a man along with them to cosign for a credit card. Getting a divorce was often difficult.

This reality led to a questioning of social norms and mores. In 1963 Betty Friedan's *The Feminine Mystique* had a profound impact on millions of women.* Women soon came together, developing consciousness-raising groups, in which they discussed their situations and found that their problems were not individual ones, but rather resulted from the second-class status of women in society. When the movement broke into public consciousness on August 26, 1970, women marched not only in New York City but also in ninety cities across the country.

Such was the origin of second-wave feminism, which came on the heels of two major social upheavals in the United States: the civil rights movement and the anti–Vietnam War movement. In 1968, the Vietnam War was raging, with over half a million US troops in Vietnam, while the mass movement of Black people for civil rights shook the country to its foundations. As mass protests around these issues escalated, youth began to radicalize. This context needs to be kept in mind when assessing feminism's second wave.

The women's liberation movement of the 1960s and early 1970s succeeded on many fronts. Looking back, it may seem hard to fully see what was accomplished—especially for those who did not live through these times. The single biggest victory was the legalization of abortion through the Supreme Court decision in *Roe v. Wade* in 1973. Avenues opened up for women in both education and career paths. Today 57 percent of women participate in the workforce. Women were able to break into "nontraditional jobs" and become electricians, machine operators, welders, and the like. In addition, women were able to pursue fields that had been limited to them previously such as law, medicine, and engineering. The word *sexism* did not even exist before the second wave. Women are com-

---

*   Betty Friedan, *The Feminine Mystique* (New York: W.W. Norton, 1963).

monly referred to as "Ms.," their marital status being irrelevant. Sexual harassment and sexual violence are now acknowledged—at least formally—to be deep-going social problems.

As women's consciousness increased, they fought back against domestic violence, as documented by Mariame Kaba in her 2014 anthology, *No Selves to Defend.* One of these women, Cassandra Peten, was charged in 1978 with assault with intent to commit murder after fighting physical abuse from her husband. Her case was taken up by organizations such as the National Association of Black Feminists with the slogan, "Clear Cassandra Peten! Defend the right of women to protect themselves from physical abuse!" After serving a sixty- to ninety-day "observation" period, she was released in 1979 on parole. Though successful, her case only reminds us that thousands more women faced physical abuse and continue to do so today.

Another major accomplishment coming out of feminism's second wave was the passage in 1972 of Title IX, which prohibited discrimination against women in any educational program receiving federal funds. Title IX had a huge impact on women in sports, in particular.

Young women at colleges and universities fought for women's studies courses and departments. In 1970, San Diego State University was the first to adopt such a course of study.

The women's movement challenged long-held views of the family—with men as the breadwinners and women as the homemakers—and raised the issue of child care as a challenge for

---

*   Mariame Kaba, ed., *No Selves to Defend: A Legacy of Criminalizing Women of Color for Self-Defense* (Chicago: Love & Protect, 2014), https://noselves2defend.files.wordpress.com.pdf.

society, not just as an individual problem. Many of the opportunities that women have today, and the cultural shifts in attitudes, can be traced to the powerful women's liberation movement of the 1960s and early 1970s.

But alongside these accomplishments, numerous criticisms of or misconceptions about the second wave of feminism have developed over the last fifty years.

One such misconception is that it was a movement exclusively of white, middle-class women. While white women were certainly the majority of some organizations, especially the more established ones like the National Organization for Women, Black women were an integral part of the movement from the beginning. The growing militancy of Black women in particular was evident during these years. Black women—triply oppressed as Black people, as women, and as workers—were able to raise specific class-based issues. They were able to point out that while many white, middle-class women could remain in the home, they needed to work outside the home to support their families. And since Black women faced special attacks from the government due to racism, they, along with Puerto Rican, Chicana, and Native American women, raised demands that spoke to their needs, such as "No forced sterilizations."

Black women, Puerto Rican women, Chicanas, and Asian American women often formed their own organizations to fight for their demands.

The National Chicana Conference, held in Houston in May 1971 was attended by six hundred women from twenty-three states. One of the workshop resolutions stated, "Free, legal abortions and birth control for the Chicano community, controlled by the Chicanas. As Chicanas, we have the right to control our own bodies."

In 1970, the Third World Women's Alliance (TWWA) was founded, whose origins came out of the civil rights movement, specifically the Student Nonviolent Coordinating Committee (SNCC), one of the major organizations in the fight for Black rights in the 1960s. Frances Beal, one of the TWWA leaders, wrote "Double Jeopardy: To Be Black and Female," which appeared among other places in Robin Morgan's *Sisterhood Is Powerful* in 1970 as well as in the book *The Black Woman* printed in 1970.* The Third World Women's Alliance began publishing the newspaper *Triple Jeopardy* in 1971.

In her book, *We Were There: The Third World Women's Alliance and the Second Wave*, published in 2021,† Patricia Romney introduces her new book by explaining that she was determined to write it due to her students' impression that women of color were absent from the movement of the 1960s and '70s. Romney interviewed thirty-three individuals involved with the TWWA. From her own experience as a member of the group and as a Black woman, she explained, "I had been a part of the movement from which women of color were supposedly absent. The Black women, *and* Latinas, *and* Asian women, *and* Middle Eastern women with whom I worked in the Alliance were in no way silent

---

*   Robin Morgan, ed., *Sisterhood Is Powerful: An Anthology of Writings from the Women's Liberation Movement* (New York: Random House, 1970); Toni Cade Bambara, ed., *The Black Woman: An Anthology* (New York: New American Library, 1970).

†   Patricia Romney, *We Were There: The Third World Women's Alliance and the Second Wave* (New York: The Feminist Press, 2021).

about their oppression as women. We were deeply involved, and we asserted our rights in vocal and active ways."

One of the people interviewed for this book, Maryanne Weathers, was both a member of Female Liberation and the Black and Third World Women's Alliance. She was the author of a far-reaching article that appeared in *No More Fun and Games* in 1969, titled "An Argument for Black Women's Liberation as a Revolutionary Force," which is reprinted in the documents section of this book. This article is used today in some women's and gender studies classes and has appeared in several anthologies.

In addition, notable Black feminist lawyer and women's rights advocate Florynce (Flo) Kennedy addressed numerous women's liberation rallies during these years, along with many other Black women. Kennedy was also the coauthor in 1971 of one of the first books on abortion, *Abortion Rap.*[*]

In 1974 Black feminists in Boston formed the Combahee River Collective. "The Combahee River Collective Statement" published in April 1977 puts it clearly: "Black, other Third World, and working women have been involved in the feminist movement from its start, but both outside reactionary forces and racism and elitism within the movement itself have served to obscure our participation."[†]

The second wave of feminism was not monolithic. Boston Female Liberation was part of its radical wing, which saw wom-

---

[*]   Florynce Kennedy and Diane Schulder, *Abortion Rap* (New York: Mc-Graw Hill, 1971).

[†]   Combahee River Collective, "The Combahee River Collective Statement," https://americanstudies.yale.edu/sites/default/files/files/Keyword%20Coalition_Readings.pdf.

en's oppression as the result of the entire structure of society. Female Liberation, as an organization, was uncompromising in its fight for women's emancipation. We knew that if we didn't fight for our rights, no one would. We acted on that belief. As readers will see throughout this book, Female Liberation made a significant contribution to radical feminist thought and action.

Female Liberation stated our aims clearly in the first issue of the *Second Wave* in spring 1971:

> Female Liberation is an organization which encompasses all aspects of feminist struggle, including education, consciousness-raising activities, and action around such basic demands of the movement as childcare, abortion and equal pay. No woman is excluded from Female Liberation who is interested in the development of a strong, autonomous women's movement capable of bringing about change on every level. It is becoming clear that this movement is reaching into every layer of the female population. We want to help mobilize the energies and power of these masses of women to fight for nothing less than our total liberation.

Many of the prominent public leaders of the movement and their organizations put forward a different perspective: their ultimate goal was to achieve a larger place within the existing social system, and their outlook tied the fight for women's rights to an electoral strategy. These lines of division marked every stage of the women's liberation movement.

Boston Female Liberation stands out sharply for both its militancy and its clarity on the nature of sexism.

Second-wave feminism was also attacked from the right wing. Slanders were hurled from the "pro-family" movement, accusing feminists of betraying the family and, among other unflattering depictions, portraying the activists as "man-haters" and "bra-burners." To some degree, aspects of these caricatures still live on in public consciousness.

≈

As we quickly learned, however, no victory is permanently secure. Each and every gain for women's rights must be defended against attempts to erode or eliminate it. Escalating attacks have occurred, in particular, around the right to obtain a safe, legal abortion.

In the document "Abortion: A Feminist Perspective," originally published in the *Second Wave* in 1971 and reprinted in the documents section of the book, Nancy Williamson states:

> The question of abortion and a woman's right to obtain one directly threatens the institutions of the family, the church, and the state; in short, the whole sexist society in which we live. We are not asking for abortion. We are asking for control of our bodies and thus our lives.

As this book is being completed, attacks on women are mounting, especially on the right to choose abortion. Numerous states have imposed restrictions and bans on the procedure, drastically restricting access, especially for poor and working-class women. The state of Texas passed a draconian bill September 1, 2021, that bans abortions after six weeks of pregnancy, at a time when most don't even know they are pregnant. Other states have begun to introduce similar bans.

The Supreme Court, in a direct challenge to *Roe v. Wade*, agreed to take up Mississippi's fifteen-week abortion ban in its 2021–22 term.

In response to these attacks, on October 2, 2021, some one hundred thousand demonstrated in six hundred and fifty cities throughout the United States in the largest single outpouring for the right to choose abortion since 2004. Noteworthy is a new generation coming to the struggle—young women and others, who have known no other world than the one in which they can obtain a safe, legal abortion. These young activists will not easily give up control over their own bodies.

Emboldened by the wave of abortion bans enacted by politicians from both major political parties, anti-abortion forces continue their harassment at clinics that offer abortions. The anti-choice right wing attempts to blockade doors to clinics, and smash windows in an effort to intimidate and frighten clinic workers, subjecting doctors and other health care workers to increasing harassment, including death threats.

The attacks on the right to abortion are part of an ideological campaign by the rulers to reverse the gains women have made in the last decades—the aim being to control us, push us back, try to convince us that our main role in society is to reproduce and be mothers. They want to establish that we alone should bear the cost of child care, that it's "OK" and "natural" for us to be paid less than men for the same work. By standing up for the right to control our own bodies, to determine when and if we will have children, we can give a resounding "NO" to this ideological campaign.

A similar ideological campaign is also directed against gays, lesbians, and trans people. Supporters of abortion rights know all too well that right-wing forces backed by the government are aiming their fire not only at the right to choose abortion, but also at the right of all people, regardless of racial or gender identity, to live a life free of harassment.

Women fighting for their rights face other challenges, among them the fact that the Equal Rights Amendment (ERA) is still not the law of the land. Having been first introduced in Congress in 1923, the amendment simply stated, "Equality of rights under the law shall not be denied or abridged by the United States or by any State on account of sex." A campaign to get the ERA ratified in the 1970s included a massive demonstration of one hundred thousand in Washington, DC, in 1978. Although the ERA enjoyed majority support in the population, the amendment failed to win ratification in face of determined opposition by opponents of women's rights.

In addition, fighting back against sexual harassment remains a major concern, as evidenced by the growth of the Me Too movement. As gender violence continues, more and more people will resist.

The lack of adequate, affordable child care remains a central challenge in our fight for equality, as highlighted by the COVID-19 pandemic. This pandemic has had a major impact on the employment of women. According to the Bureau of Labor Statistics 2021, there were 2.2 million fewer women in the paid work force in October 2020 than in October 2019. And in December 2020 alone, the Bureau of Labor Statistics reported a loss of 156,000 jobs by women, at the same time that men gained 16,000 jobs. The pandemic exacerbated the inequality felt by Black and Latina women, who lost jobs at a disproportionate rate.

Women have also played a major role in the upswing of protests against police brutality, the development of the Black Lives Matter movement, and in the immigrant rights movement.

Chanting "We Won't Go Back" and "Bans Off our Bodies," thousands of women and their allies today have taken up the banner and are continuing the struggle for women's liberation. This book aims to be a contribution to our history and can serve as both an example and an inspiration.

≈

History is important in the movement for social change, and uncovering part of the story of the second wave of feminism is a vital part of that. As far as I am aware, there is no other account that tells the full story of a radical feminist organization in the words of the women themselves. This book can thus help to bridge the generations of fighters today from those of us involved in the early days of the women's liberation movement to those joining the struggle today. Crossing that bridge strengthens us.

A number of libraries were helpful in gathering materials for this book. Many thanks go to the wonderful women who work at Northeastern University's Snell Library Archives and Special Collections Department in Boston. A special thank you to Molly Brown, the reference and outreach archivist at the Snell Library, for her work in organizing two special events for members of Female Liberation in September 2019. The Charles Deering McCormick Library of Special Collections at Northwestern University proved to be an invaluable resource, having all of the Female Liberation newsletters. In addition, the Sophia Smith Collection of Women's History at Smith College provided material, as did the Schlesinger

Library at Radcliffe College. Copies of Female Liberation's magazine the *Second Wave* were all available at the library at Northeastern Illinois University in Chicago.

I would like to acknowledge help and assistance from Rachel Cohen, Barbara Gregorich, John McDonald, Mike Taber, and Edith Taber. Howard Petrick generously provided photos for the book. Catherine Russo, who produced the documentary film, *A Moment in Her Story: Stories from the Boston Women's Movement*, gave helpful tips that were invaluable in assembling this book.[*]

Most of all, I would like to thank all of the women whose accounts appear in this book. They not only agreed to tell their stories but also worked on helping to track down others and assisted with gathering information and photos. Their inspiration and encouragement over the years it took to produce this book was invaluable. A special thank you to Boden Sandstrom for interviewing me for the book. I especially want to acknowledge Delpfine Welch, who read over and edited many different drafts of the book, providing extremely important input.

To the women of the world who are standing up and fighting back, I salute you!

Nancy Rosenstock
October 2021

---

[*]   Catherine Russo, *A Moment in Her Story: Stories from the Boston Women's Movement*. Available at catherinerussodocumentaries.com.

WOMEN INTERVIEWED

Interviews occurred from 2016 to 2019.

Claudette Begin
Dany Byrne
Ann Marie Capuzzi
Evelyn Clark
Chris Hildebrand
Ginny Hildebrand
Jeanne Lafferty
Ruthann Miller
Nancy Rosenstock
Boden Sandstrom (Barbara Reyes)*
Diana Travis
Maryanne Weathers
Delpfine Welch

---

*   During the years covered in this book, Boden's name was Barbara
Reyes.

Chapter 1

THE ROAD TO FEMINISM

The women who were interviewed for this book grew up facing a reality that was different from what young women confront today. In the 1950s and early 1960s, young women were often taught that their goal in life was to "find a man"—and then spend the rest of their days pleasing him, while bearing and raising children. Defying that role, the women here describe how they became feminists and what brought them to Boston Female Liberation, one of the most important and influential radical women's groups that arose in the second wave of feminism.

Boden: I grew up in Fairport, New York, a small country town south of Rochester in an oppressive, patriarchal family. Even though I was one of the fastest runners in my grade, my mother advised me to always let the boys win. My first political act was in the third grade when I demanded to be allowed to play touch football; I was sent home with a note.

On a scholarship, I went to a small undergraduate school, St. Lawrence University, in the northern Adirondacks of upstate New York. It was very insular and not particularly diverse, but it provided an excellent interdisciplinary education. I started out as a physics major, but later switched to literature because I could not keep up. At that time, women had curfews, and I was the only female in the class. My male classmates got together after hours to work on their lab reports, which I could not do. I was at a distinct disadvantage!

I went to graduate school at the University of Michigan in Ann Arbor from 1967 to 1968, where I got a master's degree in library science. In 1968 world-shaking events were happening. That was the year Martin Luther King Jr. was killed, and I started to become politicized. I learned about the Vietnam War and social issues such as racism. I would stand in the middle of the quad on campus and take every leaflet and flyer I could find. I even went to a Black Panther Party meeting. Thankfully, I woke up to the world around me.

My first job as a librarian was in California at San Jose State, where I met my husband, Rogelio Reyes, a Chicano (Mexican American) political folk and flamenco singer. He was active in the farmworkers movement* and was also a member of the Brown Berets, an organization of Chicanos formed in the late 1960s. Through him, I learned a lot about political movements, social injustice, and the power of music.

I didn't realize it at the time, but when I was in undergraduate school, I was very depressed. I figured out later that the root cause was being oppressed as a woman. I began to see that feminism was exactly what I needed to be a full human being.

I moved to Boston in 1970 with Rogelio and got a job as the head of the Circulation Department at Northeastern University

---

*   The struggle of the United Farm Workers of America (UFW), led by César Chavez, Dolores Huerta, and others, initiated a widely observed grape boycott in 1967 that won the support of millions throughout the country.

Library. The first thing I did politically was to seek out a feminist consciousness-raising group. At that point, I was still learning how to become a whole person and to grow individually. My memory of this group is that it was incredibly supportive. It was a wonderful step for me.

Being in the consciousness-raising group led me to want to be more active politically. That's how I became a member of Female Liberation. It was a fantastic group of women—a perfect place for me. We as a group figured out what kinds of issues we wanted to work on to advance feminism and women's rights.

Delpfine: I grew up in Salem, Massachusetts, north of Boston, and went to Catholic school from kindergarten through two years of college. From 1967 to 1969 I went to Emmanuel College, at that time a Catholic women's college in Boston, while I was living at home. I was the oldest of eight children and had a lot of family responsibilities. I was essentially a second mother. I had to drive the Sunday morning paper route, so I didn't even get to go out much on the weekend.

I was a "good girl" in high school and naive in many ways. I was active in sports, and in the student council. As I reached puberty, my mother taught me about my body, but not about sex. I had six brothers, so I knew about male anatomy. When I asked my mother where babies come from, she told me that you have a baby when you love someone. I remember in the eighth grade being afraid that I could get pregnant because I thought I loved a boy. It wasn't until my college biology class that I learned that intercourse was necessary to get pregnant. That wasn't the only thing that college opened my eyes to seeing.

At Emmanuel, we were required to wear skirts or dresses to class. That's what was expected of women at the time. I vividly remember one experience. I needed to go to a play that my brother in high school was part of. I knew that I was expected to wear a skirt, and I decided not to. I was dressed nicely in gray wool-lined pants and a mock turtleneck with a pin. I looked very respectable. But my mother freaked out. She said that I had to change into a skirt or not go to the play. This event had a big impact on me.

I also began to question the Catholic Church and the existence of God. In my sophomore year, I brought in Mary Daly to speak at Emmanuel. She was a leader in feminist theology who challenged the Catholic Church in many ways. That was my first step.

It was through my classes in sociology and anthropology that I started to question the role of women in the family and in society. In the spring of 1969, I took a sociology course called "Comparative Cultural Institutions." Despite its name, the course focused almost exclusively on the role of religion in society. What an eye-opener the course was for me. I went to the dean to tell her that I was no longer a Catholic and needed to be exempt from taking future theology classes.

Around the same time, I went to a meeting at Massachusetts Institute of Technology (MIT), where I met a woman who was a member of Cell 16. I started going to meetings at Abby Rockefeller's house, where Cell 16 was based.

In the summer of 1969, I left home quite dramatically and moved into an apartment in Somerville with two other women who were also sociology majors from Emmanuel. I remember having discussions at the house about Marxism with the women around Cell 16.

Cell 16 then moved to an office near where I lived in Somerville. I started studying Tae Kwon Do. I went from wearing skirts at school to hawking our journal, *No More Fun and Games,* in the middle of Harvard Square in a T-shirt, jeans, and bare feet!

Evelyn: I grew up in the Midwest in the 1950s. I was born into a Catholic family, and attended Catholic schools from the first grade through my third year in college. I found out the hard way that there were some serious gaps in my education when, at twenty-one, I had an unexpected pregnancy. I gave birth to a beautiful child who I gave up for adoption to a couple who were ready, willing, and able to receive him into their lives.

In 1968 I moved to Boston to be close to my brother and his wife, who had been my main and only support in my recent crisis. By being close to them I was in a position to rebuild my life.

At my first job in Boston I was fortunate enough to have two coworkers who became my friends. They introduced me to so much—to the city, to lots of people who were their friends, to the sports and music scenes, but most importantly to left-wing politics and the anti–Vietnam War movement.

Through my antiwar contacts I found out about a women's political gathering, my first. The meeting was informal and held at a private home in a Boston suburb. That's where I met Jeanne Lafferty, who, it turned out, lived two blocks from me.

Jeanne, who has been my lifelong friend to this day, was already a part of Cell 16, and that's how I was introduced and accepted into the group. That was the beginning of my feminist enlightenment—being with other women as women for our own sake, sharing our experiences, and comparing notes. Once this started, there was no stopping it. We called it consciousness-raising.

Feminism was an idea whose time had come. There truly was liberation and power in sharing our experiences and expressing feminist ideas, and this spread quickly and broadly. That's why the journals of female liberation produced by Cell 16 were so successful and in demand at that time.

Feminism healed me. It gave context to my life and my experiences. Everything about me, all my conditioning up to that point, was reordered by this new consciousness of myself.

Jeanne: I struggled when I was young with the whole issue of the situation of women. Many of us did. I was living in the suburbs of New Jersey. I was what you would call a "typical housewife." Back then, what housewives with no kids did in the suburbs was to try to find something that would take up your time and fill your life. But what takes up all your time is your misery. You can feed on this for years. I know, because I did. And some women get very fat, very lazy, very demoralized and see no way out.

I read a lot. I've always been a reader. There was nothing out there that addressed this until Betty Friedan's book, *The Feminine Mystique,* came out in 1963.

I moved to Boston in 1968. I was twenty-four years old. I remember that my husband at the time and I watched on TV the Chicago police riot at the Democratic Party convention in Chicago. We weren't students. We were looking to find like-minded people, and it wasn't that easy. Shortly afterwards, I met a woman at an anti–Vietnam War meeting, and she told me about some women organizing. I had heard about Redstockings in New York City, one of the first feminist groups, and that was very exciting.

So I went to meet these women at Roxanne Dunbar's apartment in Cambridge. It was a very small group. I put on my best clothes, a herringbone tweed suit with a skirt and pumps. I had always been taught that when you go somewhere important, you put on your best clothes. I show up and I'm a fish out of water. They were dressed in T-shirts and pants. But they were nice to me. They had been taking karate lessons, and I got involved with them.

I realized we were the underdogs of the world. I started getting my training in organizing—thinking things out, organizing, and doing it.

Ginny: I was always what was called a tomboy. I was athletic and good at physical activity. I went to a summer camp, Eagle Island Camp, in upstate New York. We carried canoes; we built fires. The camp was completely run by girls and young women. It was a wonderful experience being close to other females and being outdoors and feeling totally capable. You didn't really need to have men around.

In the fall of 1969 I was a member of Students for a Democratic Society (SDS) at Boston University (BU). Sue Katz, one of the women who I knew there, had been in California, and when she returned to Boston, she started talking about feminism. It was then that I started reading the literature, much of which was written by Meredith Tax and other women who later formed the feminist group Bread and Roses.

Feminism began to change my life. My acceptance came slowly. Could it really be that my negative view of myself was largely the product of lifelong sexist molding? Heck, I wanted to believe I was special and unique in my neuroses, not like those "other" women.

At the time, I was going to a psychiatrist, and some of my issues were those of low self-esteem. I read Simone de Beauvoir's book, *The Second Sex.** At one point she makes an analogy, as I recall, comparing the male-female relationship to two cockroaches mating. I remember bursting into tears thinking, I'm nothing but a female cockroach! I cried and cried, got over it, and read more stuff. Gradually I accepted the fact that my insecurities were not unique. After a little while, I went to my psychiatrist and said, "I'm going to stop seeing you because I now realize my problems are not individual, but they're because I'm a woman in a sexist society. I have to fight that society and its debasement of women. That's how I'll rebuild my sense of self-worth."

Feminist ideas washed over me and refreshed my youthful self-confidence and optimism, which I'd lost in my late teens. "Sisterhood is powerful" became my mantra.

In the fall of 1969 and the spring of 1970, I was involved in organizing a student-run course—the first such course ever at Boston University—called "A Radical Critique of the American Political Economy." Howard Zinn was our sponsor. We held classes on *The Origin of the Family, Private Property and the State*† by Friedrich Engels and many writings by contemporary feminists. Out of this class, Nancy Rosenstock and I helped form a women's collective, a

---

*   Simone de Beauvoir, *The Second Sex* (New York: Vintage Books, 2011).

†   Frederick Engels, *The Origin of the Family, Private Property and the State* (New York: Pathfinder Press, 1972).

consciousness-raising group. We talked about our personal problems, which turned out to have a lot of similarities. In this way, we built empathy, which we called "sisterhood."

I ended up leaving the country and living in Canada for a year. When I returned in May of 1971, I went to my first Female Liberation meeting at its office in Central Square, Cambridge.

Nancy: I grew up in an upper middle-class suburb of New York City. When I was in high school, I used to take the train to Manhattan to hang out in Greenwich Village. The train passed through Harlem. I would wonder, How come there's all this inequality?

I spent the summer of 1968 in Europe. I was in Paris right after the May–June events, when massive numbers of students and workers went on strike.* This had a huge impact on me. I would hang out in cafés on the Left Bank, and young people my age would ask me why the United States was in Vietnam. There were signs everywhere that said, "Down with US imperialism." I came back to the United States questioning things.

I got involved in the anti–Vietnam War movement and became a member of SDS while at Boston University. One of my first political acts was in the fall of 1969. In response to the young men who were being drafted into the war and who decided to

---

* The May–June 1968 events in France began with student demonstrations in Paris that were brutally attacked by police forces. Widespread solidarity with the students sparked a general strike throughout the country that was observed by over ten million workers. The revolutionary implications of the movement had a profound impact on radicalizing youth around the world.

burn their draft cards, we had a "lie-in" at Marsh Chapel on campus to prevent them from being arrested. Following the arrests of several members of the Black Panther Party in Connecticut, I, along with other SDS members from Boston, protested in New Haven to free Black political prisoners.

However, I soon was turned off by the lack of female participation in SDS. We were not doing any of the public speaking and not taking on the main responsibilities. These were all done by men.

After Ginny and I got involved in a consciousness-raising group at BU, I ended up moving to Cambridge with two other women who I met through that group. We became radical feminists. We didn't allow men in our apartment. We didn't go to some antiwar demonstrations because they were "male-dominated." We just had to totally separate ourselves from men. We'd go down to BU, a beautiful campus where the buildings were all white, and we'd spray- paint in the middle of the night, "Out of the kitchen and into the streets!" The next day, some guy would be out there rubbing it all off. But we'd be back the following night.

At the time, the issue of abortion and access to birth control was becoming the number-one concern for women. So I got involved in Female Liberation, which was the only organization in the Boston area that was doing anything about these issues. These were my formative years. They shaped who I am today.

Maryanne: I grew up in Roxbury, Massachusetts. I was involved in the Black liberation struggle. For me, Black liberation was first. I had never heard of feminism. I got hooked on feminism after meeting Roxanne Dunbar.

One day, I was at a movie by myself, and I was thoroughly engrossed in the film. I didn't notice that a man was moving closer and closer to me. He was making sounds to me. Next thing, I see some women who had been sitting in the back approach him. I didn't notice who they were and did not notice them. The next thing I know, Roxanne with her big boots kicks him. I was horrified, and I turn around and see this woman with these gigantic boots. That is how we met.

They ended up taking me back to their place and talking to me about feminism. And I'm thinking: "How does this fit in with Black liberation? Is it all white women?" But the more I listened, the more I realized they were putting voice to what I already knew. The Black liberation struggle had always been so top-heavy with men. Men did not appreciate me.

I was and still am a follower of Malcolm X. He is the only person who ever made any sense. To the day I die, I will be a feminist and a Black nationalist. *

Diana: I grew up in the South. My grandmother used to make me wear white gloves. I would dress up for Easter in my little hat and gloves. I hated that. I went to the New England Conservatory of Music from 1966 to 1970. I played the clarinet. I actually wanted

---

*   Roxanne Dunbar-Ortiz in her book, *Outlaw Woman*, (University of Oklahoma Press, 2014) describes the impact that Maryanne's following of Malcolm X had on her. She writes, "Mary Ann had been a follower of Malcolm X after he left the Nation of Islam in 1964 and until his assassination a year later. Mary Ann brought him alive again for me. She possessed hours of audiotapes she had made of him speaking."

to play the trumpet or French horn, but my mother was afraid, because only boys played those instruments. She told the teacher that I didn't have the lips to play them.

I graduated in 1970, right after the students at Kent State were killed.* We all went on strike. The administration had to mail us our diplomas. The last month of our school year we had twenty-four-hour concerts. That was our way of protesting. While I was at the conservatory, I went to a really good talk about female liberation that Abby Rockefeller gave. It was the first time I'd heard anything like this, and I was very excited. I loved it. I joined a karate class as well. I seem to remember that it was at this point that I went to Female Liberation meetings.

Claudette: I was born into an immigrant family in a large community of French Canadian Catholics in Lewiston, Maine. I was in an orphanage for a year when I was very young after my mother died. I went to private Catholic boarding schools, where the indoctrination and control was rather severe. The nuns at the elementary school decided where I would go to high school. That ended up being a school with only eleven students in Brookline, Massachusetts, near Boston. I was there on a work scholarship. This meant that I cleaned classrooms at 4:00 p.m. with the Spanish-speaking

---

*   On May 4, 1970, the Ohio National Guard killed four students and wounded nine others at Kent State University during a protest against the US invasion of Cambodia. A national student strike occurred, involving several million college and high school students. Days later police at the predominately Black Jackson State College in Mississippi opened fire on anti–Vietnam War protesters, killing two students.

women. We didn't have any opportunity to informally socialize with the other students, except in stolen moments during class, since no one was allowed to speak in our bedrooms. We were allowed to leave the school only when chaperoned. We were very protected from any counter-influence to the old-fashioned and class-oriented religious order. My main goal in graduating from high school was to not remain a bitter person.

I went to college at Emmanuel, a Catholic women's school in Boston. I had a choice of going to a different Catholic school, but I chose Emmanuel because it was an urban college. At Emmanuel, I was able to shed my bitterness at the world, and get exposed to many progressive groups and struggles, such as the Black Panthers and the anti–Vietnam War movement. Becoming a rebel myself, I easily sympathized with those I learned had been oppressed. I also found it exhilarating to participate with other women in organizing around issues that directly affected our lives. We fought for better curfews in the dorms at school and achieved dramatic changes. They kept track of us by having us sign in and out.

We had lots of discussion, initiated by Pat Galligan, about the rule that you couldn't wear pants at school. This was in 1969. We decided to say, Okay, let's fight for pants just in the library. No outsiders were allowed in the library, nor were men. We had a strike to be allowed to wear pants in the library and we won!

We achieved student-staff-faculty decision-making meetings in the sociology department. We were even able to push out a tenured monsignor professor who was a horrible teacher by convincing every single prospective student to cancel their sign-ups to his classes.

I became active at Emmanuel in the anti–Vietnam War movement. Through that I met Female Liberation.

Chris: Soon after I moved to Boston in 1966, I became involved in the anti–Vietnam War movement. My parents had been radicalizing around civil rights and I had helped them a little bit in New Jersey before I moved. When I got to Boston, the antiwar movement was heating up, and I was very, very angry about the war in Vietnam. I got involved in the Cambridge Committee to End the War in Vietnam because I ran into some people in Cambridge, in Harvard Square, who were leafleting for it. After that, I was active in the antiwar movement for quite a while, and I got involved through that in the socialist movement.

I joined Female Liberation in September 1970, following the August 26 women's rights demonstration. Being active in Female Liberation really contributed greatly to my radicalization.

Ann Marie: As soon as I heard the word "feminist," I knew that's what I was. The way I was raised by my parents was very different. I think it was when I was in the seventh grade that I started to become a rebel. It was during a math class.

The nun accused me of something. I had borrowed a dime to draw a circle for a math question, and the nun went crazy. I don't know if she thought I was cheating or what. I was up in front of the class and stated my opinion about what had happened. One of my friends defended me. The nun started pushing me out of the room. I stood there defiantly. Naturally, I had to go to the principal's office, and my mother had to pick me up at school. She was hysterical. To her, everything had to be according to the rule of the land. She kept saying, "Wait 'til your father gets home."

My father got home and took me downstairs. I told him the story. He said that what I'd done, defending myself, was a good thing. He told me that I could do anything I wanted in this world, but the one thing I could not do was lie, because then there would be no basis for human relationships. That's how I was raised.

When I was seventeen, I went into a convent in Baltimore for a year and a half. I couldn't find God in the convent. It was pretty medieval. I was very depressed and didn't know what to do. I realized that there were so many rules in the convent, and the nuns that I'd known in high school were violating those rules. Little things like asking, "Will you mail these letters for me?" But when I was in the convent, I found out that you weren't allowed to write letters except at prescribed times. I began to think: Why are people spending their lives like this? It was the hypocrisy that got me out of there. The love and forgiveness of the Jesus stories was missing in the way students were treated.

I went through fifteen years of female-only schooling—grammar school, high school, and three years of college. The college was in Baltimore: the College of Notre Dame, an all-female college. I found that to be very hypocritical too. In the middle of my junior year, I decided I needed a change. My whole life I had been involved in all-female schools, so I transferred to Fairleigh Dickinson, a co-ed college in New Jersey.

I took a world history course at Fairleigh Dickinson the summer before my senior year, and I realized that there are all these similar stories to the birth of Christ. I started to think that this was just a story. I met a Jewish boy who was rebelling against his Jewish faith. We became atheists together.

My senior year was 1963. I was a biology pre-med major. There were seven upperclasswomen in this curriculum. This new environment, a school with boys, was the first time I realized that I was oppressed as a woman. All-female schools were supportive and equal. I didn't realize how oppressive things could be until I started going to schools with boys. It was very competitive, and the only boys who talked to me were the ones who wanted to copy my homework. Two women graduated before me, and they were both 4.0 students. One of them got into medical school even before the boys did, but the school wanted her parents to contribute big-time financially. Her family didn't have any money, so she couldn't go to med school. Out of these seven women, no one actually went to medical school.

I lived in Providence, Rhode Island, in 1969. I worked with a woman who was going to school at Brown University to form a women's center. We organized the first Women against the War march and rally in Providence. Florence Luscomb, a suffragist who lived in Boston, was one of the speakers at the rally.

In the spring of 1971, I lived in San Diego where I participated in forming the first San Diego Women's Center and was elected to its member coordinating committee.

I joined Female Liberation in June 1971.

Chapter 2

SWEPT UP BY A WAVE

In the years 1968–1970, some of the main activities of the organization included publishing the journal No More Fun and Games; *studying self-defense; joining with others in the first Congress to Unite Women in 1969; and participating in the rising gay liberation movement. Originally called Female Liberation, it was renamed Cell 16 in 1969. Both names were used until the fall of 1970, when Female Liberation and Cell 16 became separate organizations.*

Jeanne: I met Female Liberation in 1968. At that time, the other women I remember were Roxanne Dunbar and Abby Rockefeller. Later, I got connected with Delpfine Welch, Evelyn Clark, and Pat Galligan.

We used to hang out at Abby's house. She had the equipment to put out the literature in her basement. Delpfine, Evelyn, Pat, and I were the worker-bees in the basement. We did all the grunt work.

In 1969 we became Cell 16. The whole concept behind Cell 16 was that radical cells would develop. We were supposed to tell interested women to go form their own cells.

Delpfine: I met Cell 16 in 1969 during my sophomore year at Emmanuel College. At that time, Abby Rockefeller, Jayne West, and Dana Densmore were all taking self-defense classes. I also remember the political discussions we had about the issues affecting women—abortion and child care.

Evelyn: In the beginning, Cell 16 met regularly in the apartment of one of the members in Central Square, Cambridge. It was very informal. For me, it was exciting and a bit intimidating. It was a small and diverse group of women, all of whom were powerful in their own right: Betsy Warrior, an activist welfare mother; Abby Rockefeller, a philanthropist; Dana Densmore, an intellectual and outdoor adventurer; Roxanne Dunbar, a social activist and writer; Jayne West, a young skillful master of Tae Kwon Do; Lisa Leghorn, a student who wrote articles for the journal; and Hilary Langhorst, an artist and writer.

I was not interested in writing, but I found my niche working with the journals—selling them at events and managing their distribution. We sent a lot out to people through the mail. The excitement for me was witnessing the incredible demand for the literature. It was common to sell out at events and demonstrations. That was very satisfying. Women were so hungry for this information. It was like being swept up by a wave.

Nancy: In 1969 when I was a student at Boston University, I remember that many of the articles written by leaders of Cell 16 were reprinted by the New England Free Press. I still have some of them today, including an article by Betsy Warrior on "Females and Welfare" and one by Roxanne Dunbar on "Poor White Women."

One article in particular that was written by Jeanne Lafferty, "Pass the Word," had a big impact on me at the time. It argued that the word "female" is a better, more scientific, word to use than "woman." The article states: "It might be more sensible to question the word 'woman,' which has social implications and innuendos. It often implies that to fulfill the requirements of one's sex is an achievement rather than a given biological fact. Somewhere in the process of striving for the rewards offered to 'good women,' we became aware of our humiliating role as men's willing victims."

No More Fun and Games

In October 1968 the first issue of a "journal of female liberation" was published in Boston. Writing in 1969 after the second printing of the journal, the women involved explained that the first issue, which was untitled, represented our "first thoughts" and "our intense rage, isolation and even fear. We were not certain that a movement would develop, much less a social revolution. We did know that we were determined to stand and fight, even if we were alone." Later the journal was titled No More Fun and Games. As one of the early feminist journals with original writings, it became influential. Requests for copies of the journal poured in from women all over the world. One reader from New Haven, Connecticut, wrote, "Please send us the journals. I like your journal very much and so does the rest of New Haven Women's Liberation." The West Side Women's Center in Milwaukee requested copies. From France, a woman wrote in, "I found the journal exhilarating."

Dany: I was instinctively drawn to feminism. The journal *No More Fun and Games,* to me at the time, was really transformative. Lots of people read the journal as an introduction to feminist thought.

Boden: I remember reading *No More Fun and Games.* I was totally impressed with the women's thinking. It contained not only articles on the political and social analysis of sexism, sexuality, and racism, but was interspersed with poetry, photographic collages, and drawings.

Delpfine: One of the things I did when I was involved with Cell 16 was to sell *No More Fun and Games* on the street. I especially remember being in Harvard Square with bundles of the journal. We were out there every day. The Black Panther Party sold their newspaper in Harvard Square, and we would sell next to them. We became friends and political allies.

Maryanne: I wrote an article in February 1969 that appeared in the second issue of *No More Fun and Games,* "An Argument for Black Women's Liberation as a Revolutionary Force." The article said in part: "Black women are clearly the most oppressed and degraded minority in the world. Why can't we rightfully claim our place in the world? We women must start this thing rolling."

In May 1969, Cell 16 and other feminists organized the New England Regional Female Liberation Conference. It was held at Emmanuel College and was attended by over six hundred people.

Delpfine: I was involved with procuring space at Emmanuel College for the New England Regional Female Liberation Conference with help from my roommate, who was vice president of the student council. Dozens of workshops were held: Black Women in a Caste Society; Advertising and Media as Oppressors of Females; Working Women; Family as the Basic Unit of Female Oppression; Strategy and Tactics for a Female Liberation Movement; and others.

A significant development came out of the "Women and Their Bodies" workshop, which continued to meet after the conference adjourned. These women put together a book originally called *Women and their Bodies.* Later, in 1971, they changed the name to *Our Bodies, Ourselves.* The book was widely circulated and respected.

Defying Standards of Beauty and Femininity

Delpfine: I remember wearing wide leather belts and men's corduroy pants. Men's pants were all we could find that were simple, comfortable, and had pockets. There just wasn't anything available for women that wasn't frilly. We wanted just basic pants. We attempted to look asexual—consciously trying to be neither

---

* Boston Women's Health Collective, *Our Bodies, Ourselves,* 1970; republished by Simon and Schuster in multiple editions between 1973 and 2011. See also https://www.ourbodiesourselves.org/our-story/.

male nor female. It was harder for me because I was big-busted. I remember finding a minimizing-type bra and wearing that. One time I was hitchhiking from Watertown on the main drag right near where I lived, dressed in a stocking cap and a red and black lumber jacket. A man stopped and said, "Where are you going, son?" When he realized that I wasn't a boy, he exclaimed, "Wait 'til I tell my wife about this!"

I remember picking up a fabulous black leather motorcycle jacket at a thrift shop, which I eventually gave to my roommate.

I did not shave my legs until much later, when I took a summer job in the corporate world. We also didn't shave under our arms.

There was a lot of pressure to cut our hair. I didn't agree and did not cut my hair until later. It didn't make sense to me. In 1969 my hair was long. I later had short hair. But I did not cut it in any symbolic way.

Boden: I remember we used to buy our clothes at the army/navy surplus store in Cambridge. I cut my hair short for the first time in my life; it was totally liberating.

Nancy: My roommates and I would dress in absolutely crazy outfits—striped pants, plaid tops, and combat boots. Then we'd walk through Harvard Square!

The *Second Wave* featured an article by Nancy Williamson, "The Case for Studied Ugliness." It was a great article that challenged society's standards of "beauty" and "femininity." It stated:

> Women in the movement are frequently accused of being
> ugly (as if it were some crime that invalidates everything

else we do), of defeminizing ourselves (femininity being directly proportional to the shape, size and amount of breasts and legs showing), of having an uncouth appearance (i.e. short hair, shiny noses, unshaved legs and armpits). Frequently at public forums, orientation meetings, and in personal contacts, we are questioned about our appearance. Why do you wear "men's clothes?" is a frequent query. (Anything that is comfortable seems to be classified as "men's clothes.") Why don't you want to look attractive? (It seems we can't be attractive if we don't wear makeup and dresses.)

Jeanne: I attended the first Congress to Unite Women in New York City in November 1969. It drew five hundred women. It was one of the first national women's liberation conferences. At that time, I was in Cell 16. We were invited on stage to do a presentation. We decided to do something that would knock the socks off the whole room. So we put one of our young members with beautiful long hair on a chair on the stage, and then we proceeded to cut her hair off. The crowd was in an uproar, screaming "No, no, no!"

At that time, many people in the audience saw this as if we were stripping her of her femininity. That's what the response was about. We did it precisely to get that response—to raise consciousness.

Evelyn: The Congress to Unite Women was initiated by the National Organization for Women (NOW) and was held to create a coming together of moderate and radical feminist interests.

This was very early—November 23, 1969.

The conference lasted the entire weekend. When Female Liberation, along with other groups, was offered the opportunity to give a presentation on the last day of the conference, we wanted to do it, but didn't know exactly what we were going to do. We were all staying at the Chelsea Hotel, and we brainstormed together in one of our rooms on Saturday night. A random comment by Roxanne about Jeanne's curly, red hair and how attractive hair is to men led us into an examination of the role women's hair has played throughout history, how the "feminine image" has been a tool of our oppression, and how we still identified ourselves with it.

Before the night was over, many of us, including myself, had let someone cut our long hair short as an act of liberation. We decided that for our presentation Lisa Leghorn, who was a young student who had very long, wavy, beautiful hair, would have her hair cut on stage. Either Lisa or the person cutting her hair spoke about what they were doing and why. I do remember the audience was incredulous and audibly gasped when Lisa's hair was cut. It was a very creative and powerful moment for us, individually and as a group.

Ann Marie: I had been living in San Diego and I called my good friend, Chris Hildebrand, who was in Boston. She said, "Oh, you have to come to Boston because we have Female Liberation. It's so wonderful." I got off the phone and told my boyfriend we were going back to Boston. He replied, "Have you been talking to your dyke friend?" After hearing that, I picked up the scissors and cut off all my long, brown hair to protest what he had just said.

I had to get a job when I moved back to Boston. I hadn't shaved my legs in a few years. I shaved them, put on a skirt and pantyhose, and went to a job interview for a clerical position in Cambridge. When I walked into the Female Liberation office, Jeanne Lafferty started laughing hysterically, and kept pointing to the back of my legs. It turns out that I'd shaved my legs with the pantyhose on the floor, catching all the hair. When I pulled them up, all the hair got stuck on the back of my legs. I'd gone to the job interview like that! Of course, I didn't get the job.

Self-Defense

The women of Cell 16 believed that women should be able to defend themselves. The third issue of No More Fun and Games, *which came out in November 1969, included a statement that pointed out: "We must learn to fight back. It must become as dangerous to attack a woman as to attack another man. We will not be raped! We will not be chewed upon! We will not be slashed! We will not be 'treated rough' by any man, 'brute' or pervert. We will not be leered at, smirked at, or whistled at by men enjoying their private fantasies of rape and dismemberment."*

Delpfine: Shortly after getting involved with Cell 16 in 1969, I started taking Tae Kwon Do. I was good at it, as I had always been athletic. It got me back in shape. I was taking the classes along with Jeanne Lafferty, Pat Galligan, Abby Rockefeller, Jayne West, Dana Densmore, and others.

When Jayne and Abby started out, they were the only

women in the class. They got the instructor to start another class for women only. I went to both classes. When I was in the mixed class, I was very competitive with the men. I remember trying (and succeeding!) not to fail first when holding a push-up on my knuckles.

I remember how good it felt knowing how to defend myself. I could walk down the street exuding strength and confidence, aware of the space around me. Being able to feel like that was a big part of what self-defense is all about.

We traveled to campuses in the Boston area giving Tae Kwon Do demonstrations. Pat Galligan and I distributed a leaflet that we wrote in 1969, "Females and Self-Defense," at three Boston women's colleges—Emmanuel, Simmons, and Wheelock. The third issue of *No More Fun and Games* printed the leaflet, which states: "Women's physical weakness and its psychological consequences can only be overcome through developing their bodies. The attacks on women will stop only when it becomes as dangerous to attack a woman as it is to attack another man."

Jeanne: Self-defense was huge. We needed to defend ourselves. We also needed to show women that it's possible to take care of ourselves. It was a wonderful thing. When we got really good, we would travel around giving demonstrations to women. It was a very powerful thing to see a woman kick her leg out in that uniform and snap. That was WOW!

We traveled all over, not just in the Boston area, but also to colleges in New York and Vermont. Someone would sponsor us, and we'd put up the stage and do the karate demonstration. Then we would sit on the stage and have endless discussions with the women who came. It gave women the idea that they can be powerful.

Delpfine: I did a karate demonstration with Pat Galligan in Pittsburgh in September 1970. An article in the *Pittsburgh Post-Gazette* reported on it: "Bearing knapsacks and wearing shirts that buttoned in the male direction and corduroy pants, the Boston Karate Team of Delpfine Welch and Pat Galligan arrived in town yesterday to participate in a two-day 'Symposium on Feminism' at the University of Pittsburgh. The girls, who wear short-cropped haircuts and no make-up, demonstrated karate last night at the Pitt Student Union and spoke on 'The Need for Self-Defense.'"

Evelyn: Neither Jeanne nor I had a car. We got around on foot and public transportation. The experience of being talked at, yelled at, stared at, whistled at, pinched, poked, or followed in some form was an everyday occurrence for us and for most women who traveled in public. It was necessary to always be alert to who was around you. So the idea of self-defense was intriguing. Another dark layer of conditioning, a rather deep one, crumbled under the revelation that a woman could actually defend herself physically.

Jeanne and I began studying Tae Kwon Do. Jayne West introduced us to the studio where she studied, and they set us up with our own women's class. It was a serious and disciplined training and was physically and psychologically transformative. It increased my confidence. My body language and demeanor changed and I attracted much less negative attention on the street.

Part of learning to defend ourselves was not to act in a way to attract the attention we didn't want on the street. This led to a radical change in wardrobe, from feminine to gender-neutral—jeans, T-shirts, pea coats, and work boots. At that moment, it was very liberating to walk away from the burden of the feminine image. Jeanne and I had a lot of fun with it.

Cell 16 was one of only a few voices raising the issue of violence against women at that time.

Boden: I went to Tae Kwon Do classes as well. We had a really good time, and it was very hard work. We were excited because we were becoming stronger. We actually used the skills. We were walking home one time—I think we had been putting up posters on telephone poles—and some guys started following us and harassing us. I think it was Delpfine—she was the best, very skilled—she threatened these guys with her skills and they fled. We were getting more and more sure of ourselves and felt like we could conquer the world.

Dany: I was a member of the George Washington University women's liberation group in Washington, DC. My introduction to Female Liberation came from the women from Boston, eleven of them, who were at the George Washington University Women's Liberation Conference held in November 1970. As part of the conference, the Boston women held a karate demonstration that was well received. Some of us had already begun to study self-defense. The conference and the karate demonstration helped to get some interest going in our group.

Dana Densmore gave a talk at the conference "On Unity,"

which was later printed in the journal, *No More Fun and Games*. In the article Densmore said, "The women's movement is the most revolutionary movement that has ever come along, and its mission and duty is to fight the oppression of women as women, to fight for control over our lives: for dignity and autonomy as human beings."[*]

Later, I moved to Boston to become a member of Female Liberation.

Gay Liberation and Sexuality

Chris: In the early days of Cell 16, Dana Densmore wrote an article titled "On Celibacy" that appeared in the first journal. It says in part: "This is a call not for celibacy but for an acceptance of celibacy as an honorable alternative, one preferable to the degradation of most male-female relationships. But, it is only when we accept the idea of celibacy completely that we will ever be able to liberate ourselves."

This article and the ideas raised in it proved valuable as a consciousness-raising topic for discussion.

Diana: I found at first that the other women were not interested in gay liberation. Daughters of Bilitis (DOB), of which I was a member, first started organizing before the Stonewall Uprising on Christopher Street in New York City, which was in June of 1969.[†]

---

[*] Dana Densmore, "On Unity," *No More Fun and Games*, no. 5 (July 1971).

[†] The Stonewall Uprising is seen as marking the public emergence of

This uprising was the spark that began the fight for gay rights. After that, all of a sudden, eleven different gay organizations in Boston sprouted up. It was just amazing. Before, it had been just DOB and the Mattachine Society, which was the male group.

The first gay liberation demonstration we organized had thirty-five people at it. We smashed a wooden closet as a symbol of coming out.

We went to New York City to visit the Daughters of Bilitis chapter there, and asked them how we could do something in Boston. It was a struggle. The chapter in New York suggested we put an ad for *The Ladder*, which was their publication, in *Boston After Dark*, and in that way we could probably get some names from people who would want to subscribe to the magazine.

I went to *Boston After Dark* and asked them if they would publish our ad for *The Ladder*, and they said absolutely not. They said they had a rule that they will not do anything concerning homosexuality.

The guy from *Boston After Dark* said he would help to get us on a morning talk radio show and get some publicity. He advertised it every day for a week prior to us coming on. Two of us went on the show. We walked in and there were all these men from the Mattachine Society. We had a really great talk show that included a lot of hostile calls. We advertised our meeting, which

---

the gay liberation movement. In the early hours of June 28, 1969, police raided the Stonewall Inn in New York City's Greenwich Village. Police raids were a common form of harassment against bars that gay people flocked to. But on this night, the actions of both regular cops and riot police were met with an uprising that sparked days of street battles and demonstrations involving thousands of people.

was going to be at Trinity Episcopal Church, where, interestingly enough, the minister from where I grew up in Charlotte was now the minister. So he agreed to let us have the meeting there. Seventy women showed up! The publisher of *Boston After Dark* heard about our discussion and changed their policy.

So along with a few others, we formed the first chapter of Daughters of Bilitis in Boston. We grew to probably over a hundred members over a short period of time.

I became vice president and then president of Daughters of Bilitis and started to see that this was a bigger issue.

Chapter 3

AUGUST 26, 1970–WOMEN'S STRIKE FOR EQUALITY

On August 26, 1970, fifty years after the Nineteenth Amendment granting women the right to vote, fifty thousand marched down New York City's Fifth Avenue. "Women's Strike for Equality" demonstrations took place in ninety cities with three demands:

- *Free abortion on demand—no forced sterilization*
- *Free, community-controlled, twenty-four-hour child care centers*
- *Equal opportunities in jobs and education*

Given the central importance of August 26 to the rise of the second wave of feminism—and to Boston Female Liberation in particular—included below is an account of the New York march by its coordinator, Ruthann Miller, who was interviewed for this book.

Ruthann: I had been involved in the anti–Vietnam War movement, and in 1969 I joined a small women's consciousness-raising group in New York City called Redstockings. That year, a class-action lawsuit was filed aimed at overturning the New York law that made abortion a crime. Several groups, including Redstockings, came together to support this lawsuit. Those groups met and called a demonstration to support the case just before it went before the court. I was asked to take on the job of organizing a demonstration and the coalition, People to Abolish Abortion Laws (PAAL). That's how I became involved.

That first demonstration was in February 1970. There were five thousand people who came. It was considered a huge success.

Due to my role in organizing the February 1970 action, I was invited by Betty Friedan to come to a meeting at her house to organize for August 26, 1970. There were five people at the meeting: Betty Friedan; Ivy Bottini, who was president of the National Organization for Women at the time; Judy White, who was a representative of the Socialist Workers Party; Rita Mae Brown* and me.

Friedan had proposed the August 26 demonstration to NOW, and they had originally voted it down. Later, as things progressed, NOW endorsed the march. Those of us at the meeting at Friedan's house called for another meeting of the coalition in New York that had been working on the case for legal abortion. The idea was to have Friedan make a proposal for the August 26 demonstration to that coalition. We made the proposal, and it passed overwhelmingly. This was in March 1970. Friedan told me that she wanted me to be the coordinator of the coalition and the demonstration, because I was to her a representative of radical young women.

Since I had a little baby that I was home taking care of, Friedan made a separate proposal that she would personally arrange to raise funds for my child-care expenses, so that I could be on

---

*   Rita Mae Brown is a feminist writer, best known for her autobiographical novel *Rubyfruit Jungle*.

staff. She really didn't have to do this. I would have done it no matter what anyone said. I was on full time, 24/7 until August 26. First we worked out of an office in the West 4th Street Church in Greenwich Village; then, as we needed more space, we rented a loft on Broadway. Finally, Friedan proposed that we move to the headquarters of the Democratic Party, uptown.

We started organizing for August 26, and we got support everywhere: Church Women United; suburban women; university women; stockbrokers—all types of women. Friedan did her best to get support from every segment of the Democratic Party. All of the parts came together, and it was really astonishing. Still, we were surprised by the size of the demonstration.

On August 26, among the many tasks I had was to be in charge of the marshals. As we were assembling, the police commander came over to me and insisted that we march on the sidewalk, and he kept saying, "Hey, lady." I was at first trying to be my quiet, usual, polite self, but I got so exasperated that finally I said, "Please, just turn around and look behind you." I made a gesture pointing to the crowd. People around me started chanting, "Look behind, look behind!" The commander turned his head and saw these thousands of women, and within two seconds he gave the order to block off the street. We had permits—we had sat down with the police, the mayor—we had done all the right things. But they thought it was just going to be a couple of "girls" parading down Fifth Avenue!

The August 26 coalition continued after the demonstration. I remained on staff full time until the end of January 1971. I traveled around, baby in tow, speaking on women's liberation and abortion.

The coalition continued to debate whether we should fight for legal abortion only or whether we should continue to fight for the three agreed-upon demands. The coalition called a demonstration for the end of December around the issue of child care. But between August and December this fragile coalition, which had worked together despite many differences, started to fall apart. There were a lot of pressures on the movement, some of them from the outside, since it was suddenly discovered that this was in fact a movement. A lot of arguing and debating resulted from this. Some people broke away and left the coalition. The coalition's newsletter turned into *Ms.* magazine and became famous.

Through the women's movement—not just the demonstration but also definitely the consciousness-raising group—I became very self-confident, very sure of myself, very able, very capable, very assertive—not aggressive, but assertive. I actually believed that anything I set my mind to and worked hard at, I could figure out a way of doing. The women's movement showed me what I could do.

I was probably the least-equipped person to be in the position I was in, but sometimes in life you're just dropped somewhere. When I think back, I wonder: Did I really do that? I was a naive Irish Catholic woman from Brooklyn who had gone to Catholic schools. I was also a ballet dancer. And here I was, involved in a really exciting political time. The end result was greater than we could have imagined.

August 26 in Boston

In Boston, five thousand marched on August 26. Female Liberation was a part of the coalition that organized the demonstration.

Chris: Female Liberation became the leading activist wing of the coalition building for August 26 in Boston. I participated in the building of the demonstration that NOW had initiated. They had invited all women to be involved. It was a non-exclusionary coalition. I helped out on the day of the demonstration, as well. It was held at lunchtime at the Government Center to maximize participation from those who worked in the area. The demonstration was very successful.

For the first time in a local women's rights action, there was a gay women's liberation presence in the march. Diana Travis and others were present with a banner. Afterwards, we had a huge party at the Female Liberation office. It was just magnificent. Diana and others from the gay liberation movement were at the party, and we let them know they were welcome in Female Liberation. We started talking with NOW and others about the need to go further and continue the momentum.

After August, Female Liberation emerged as central to the women's movement in Boston. We were looked to as leaders, especially by the younger women who were becoming feminists.

Delpfine: I was the chief marshal for the August 26 demonstration in Boston. It was so exciting to look out at the sea of women (and some men) and see the signs that they were carrying: "Free Abortion on Demand, No Forced Sterilization" was one I clearly remember. The rally opened with the first speaker saying, "God has given us a beautiful day ... hasn't She?" The crowd went wild. They had never heard anything like that before. Even my mother was there with my three youngest brothers.

Ruthann: Several months after the August 26 demonstration, I went to Boston and spoke at an abortion rights rally in October 1970 at City Hall Plaza.

I had been familiar with Boston Female Liberation, and I just loved them. The general knowledge in New York at the time was that Female Liberation represented the more theoretical branch of the movement. They were like the gurus of the movement.

I was often attacked for being both a feminist and a socialist. So when some of the women from Female Liberation also became socialists, it vindicated the idea that feminism and socialism were compatible.

August 26's Impact: A New Direction

Female Liberation members in their vast majority endorsed a new direction of the organization, turning toward big opportunities to build a large, radical feminist organization, oriented to mass action. A small minority of women, including many of the original members, embarked on a different course and continued as Cell 16.

Evelyn: In August 1970, we set up an office on Boylston Street in the building of our Tae Kwon Do studio. I was the office manager, on full time.

There were two things that were important—the distribution of our literature at events and the sending out of our literature through the mail. I was responsible for both the mailing list and the bank account.

Jeanne: Once we had the new office on Boylston Street, we began to reach out, meeting women, and we grew. We attracted upwards of forty women to meetings.

I began to have questions about the way Cell 16 was organized. We were supposed to tell interested women to go form their own group or cell. I came to the realization that the cell structure was totally counter to the idea of inclusion. I began to understand more, and I thought that there are different ways of doing these things.

One night, there were all these women in the office, and we were talking about what we were doing. Suddenly, a couple of the original leaders walked in. I thought to myself, the shit's going to hit the fan, and it did. All hell broke loose. They were fit to be tied, because this was supposed to be a cell—with just so many people in it—and here there were all these people in the room. They were furious.

We weren't interested in getting into a fight, but we were going our separate ways politically, that's for sure. We were just reaching out to women. We had the office, the stamps, the envelopes, and the telephone. We had the whole thing. We were not an oppositional group or anything. We were the worker bees, like we always had been, the ones doing all the work.

Evelyn: When the political differences came to the fore, things happened very quickly. Nobody knew exactly what was going to happen, how far it was going to go, or how deep it was.

Jeanne: One night around 9:00 p.m., I was in the office by myself, and all of a sudden some people, men, barge in. They said, "This is ours and we're taking everything out of here!" All I could do was protect people's personal property. For example, I said, "You can't take that typewriter, because it belongs to Barbara Reyes [Boden Sandstrom]." They didn't know what to do, so they left it.

They tried to get the keys from our super. But since he had never seen them before, he didn't give them the keys. They were furious.

Boden: I lived in Roxbury, up on Fort Hill, in a big old town house on the third floor. I remember coming home one day and the downstairs door was open. I had been storing copies of the journal in the stairwell of the house. I came home and the journals were gone. Someone had come in and taken them. It was quite shocking.

I remember we had a lot of phone calls at the time, and a lot of meetings to figure out what to do.

Claudette: When I met Delpfine and Pat, fellow students at Emmanuel College, in the spring of 1970, I was puzzled about why they hadn't thought to tell me about Female Liberation, since I had been active at college in every struggle I had become aware of. I learned it was Female Liberation's small-group approach at that time. I was thrilled that the majority of Female Liberation members had recently decided the time was ripe to open up to include any and all women. It was also key to me that Female Liberation linked our issues to many other struggles for major social change.

Chapter 4

BEYOND OUR EXPECTATIONS

Following on the heels of the successful August 26, 1970, women's rights demonstration, Female Liberation continued to reach out to and attract new women to the organization. This chapter outlines the activities that Female Liberation was involved in during the years 1970–72.

Weekly open, democratic meetings began. Our newsletter reached a mailing list of one thousand. We also established a new magazine, the Second Wave: A Magazine of the New Feminism.

In addition, Female Liberation carried out a host of other activities designed to attract and draw new women into action. Students set up campus chapters at both Boston University and Northeastern University. Among the places where speakers from Female Liberation went were high schools and YWCAs. Jeanne Lafferty, a leader of Female Liberation, was invited to speak at a women's liberation conference in Seattle in January 1971.

Female Liberation organized a panel discussion on the Equal Rights Amendment. We held a successful speaking engagement for Anaïs Nin, a French Cuban American writer whose diaries were popular at the time.

The meeting was held at the Old Cambridge Baptist Church in Harvard Square on May 28, 1971, and was attended by 1,100 people—her largest audience ever.

Female Liberation worked on a child care referendum that appeared on the Cambridge, Massachusetts, ballot in November 1971.

The New England Women's Coalition (NEWCO), of which Female Liberation was a part, continued the work of the August 26 coalition. Several activities outlined in this chapter were successful and serve as an example of what can be accomplished when different women's groups come together around a common goal.

Female Liberation members also participated in demonstrations of the emerging gay liberation movement with their banner and bundles of the Second Wave.

One of the first activities following August 26, 1970, was a conference that Female Liberation hosted at Boston University.

Chris: Following the successful demonstration in August, Female Liberation began setting up tables on campuses throughout Boston with the journals and other literature.

At Boston University, we set up a table during registration and attracted students who wanted to start a Female Liberation chapter on their campus. They then initiated the conference in November of 1970 and got sponsorship from the university.

The Female Liberation conference at BU drew five hundred people. Other groups were invited, and there were a number of speakers. We put up posters and leaflets everywhere. The conference was great. Friday night we showed a feminist film in the big auditorium. We also had a karate demonstration. There were workshops on all different subjects: high school women, Black and Third World women, the family and female oppression, and whether feminism is revolutionary, to name just a few.

We started developing a program. We had a mass-action approach: build the women's movement. That's what we were trying to do.

Delpfine: At the BU conference, I was part of a demonstration of Tae Kwon Do . I remember demonstrating the horse stance, but instead of saying "horse," my Boston accent kicked in, and I said "hoss," to the audience's amusement.

I remember seeing my mother in the audience. After I left home, she did a 180-degree turn and became active in a group called Northshore Feminists.

≈

The office of Female Liberation became an organizing center complete with books, pamphlets, buttons, and posters.

Chris: Evelyn found the office in Central Square, Cambridge. It was very small. The room wasn't even big enough to have meetings, because now we were growing. We would meet out in the hallway. The office emptied out into this huge hallway, and at night nobody was in the building. We put out folding chairs in the hallway and had meetings there. We started a new magazine, the *Second Wave.*

Evelyn: We wrote and mimeographed a newsletter of several pages that came out every Friday. We had a very large mailing list, so volunteers would come to the office and help fold and staple it. We had a lot of fun doing this. The newsletter was key to building Female Liberation, and to building the activities of the women's movement as a whole.

Nancy: I remember the office in Central Square on the second floor. We would go up there and put out the newsletter. I remember having bundles of the *Second Wave* and selling them at various places. I had an apartment in Central Square, so I would walk from my apartment to the office. Evelyn was the office manager. I remember Chris giving the organization a lot of clarity in terms of pushing for action. We weren't just a talk group. We had to do stuff. We were a model of what's possible. We went beyond just the consciousness-raising stage, where we just talked about our oppression, to doing something about it.

Boden: What I remember from our meetings is that we all picked things to be involved in. It was an electrifying time. We were living what we had discovered in our consciousness-raising groups—that we could change our lives together. The personal was political.*

≈

---

*   The phrase "the personal is political" was a common expression of second-wave radical feminists. It comes from an article of the same name by Carol Hanisch that appeared in *Notes from the Second Year: Women's Liberation* in 1970. In consciousness-raising groups at the time, women discovered that their "problems" were not personal but stemmed from women's oppression in society.

A women's dance was organized, one of the first in Boston.

Boden: Evelyn and I, at least, and probably someone else, would often meet at a deli by the Female Liberation office early in the morning. It was wonderful. We were so excited and happy to see each other. We loved the men we were with at the time, but we were so excited about being women; being together; changing ourselves; our future; and working on women's rights.

One of these mornings, we decided to hold a women's dance. I'm pretty sure it was one of the first all-women's dances in Boston. We had it at my house in Roxbury. The third-floor apartment where Rogelio and I lived was huge. It was in a double-wide town house perched on Fort Hill. I remember that I asked Rogelio if he would not come home that night because we didn't know how long the dance would go. He was so supportive. I don't know where he went, but he stayed away all night. It was absolutely electric and amazing. We danced all night to Aretha Franklin. There were these big bay windows in the parlor, out of which you could see the lights of Boston. The ballroom had a working fireplace in it. It was very magical and a lot of fun. It almost did last all night!

≈

Students established campus chapters of Female Liberation at both Northeastern University and Boston University.

Ginny: In 1971, I got a job in the sociology department at Boston University where I had been a student from 1967 to 1970. I did this so I could be a campus activist. Along with Pat Putnam, who was a student, and others we set up a satellite chapter of Female Liberation at BU. We would set up literature tables, and we got a budget for our group through the student union. We also had a list of demands: a full-time gynecologist at the university health center, a women's center, a female studies program, and a free self-defense course for credit in the physical education program.

Nancy: In the spring of 1971, Female Liberation sponsored a course as part of BU's Communiversity. Some of the class topics were: "The Nature of Sexism," "Marriage and the Family," "Sexuality," and "Feminism as Revolutionary Theory."

≈

The rise of second-wave feminism brought to light the fact that the Equal Rights Amendment was not the law of the land. The effort to get the ERA ratified as part of the US Constitution had been something that NOW had been involved in.

Nancy: In October 1970, having not yet taken a position on this important issue, Female Liberation organized a panel discussion titled, "Women's Liberation and the Equal Rights Amendment." The speakers at the forum were: Jane Pollock, president of the eastern Massachusetts chapter of NOW; Charlene Mitchell, former presidential candidate of the Communist Party, USA; Sarah Lovell from the Socialist Workers Party; and a representative of Bread and Roses. The forum was publicized with a leaflet that posed some of the questions that at the time were prevalent: Will passage of the ERA benefit females? Should the women's movement support the ERA and if so, how? Should we favor a military draft for females?

Chris: Having worked with NOW to build August 26, we realized that Female Liberation had to take a position on the ERA. We organized a debate, and afterward, at a business meeting, Female Liberation voted to support the ERA.

≈

Female Liberation published a magazine, the Second Wave: A Magazine of the New Feminism. *It included news stories, poetry, fiction, graphics, and articles expressing a wide range of feminist thought and viewpoints. Many women contributed articles to the magazine including Mary Daly, an outspoken Catholic who was pro-choice; and Barbara Roberts, a doctor who was a strong supporter of abortion rights.*

Chris: I remember an example of the national influence of Female Liberation. Before *Ms.* magazine was established, Gloria Steinem, who was in town to speak at a public meeting in Boston that many of us attended, met with us to find out about our magazine, the *Second Wave.** At her request we met up at the airport, and she questioned us about our magazine and offered suggestions.

Another time Steinem came to Boston to help businesswomen who were trying to gain admission to a local restaurant where many businessmen ate lunch and made contacts and

---

*   Gloria Steinem, feminist leader, founded *Ms.* magazine in 1972.

deals. Women had been excluded, and this hurt their careers. Steinem invited Female Liberation to join with NOW members and her other contacts. We all marched up to the restaurant and attempted to enter for lunch. The press had been invited to witness the action. The management at first tried to exclude us on the basis that we were female, but due to the press being there, they told Gloria that she and the rest of us couldn't enter because we were wearing slacks, never appropriate attire in their formal dining room. When Gloria told them that we would all take off our slacks so we could get in, they relented and we were seated. We ended up having a nice lunch and conversed about the women's movement.

≈

The New England Women's Coalition held a meeting at Boston University on February 6, 1971, and planned three events:

- *A demonstration on March 23, 1971, around the slogans: "free abortion on demand, repeal all abortion laws—no forced sterilization."*
- *A New England Congress to Unite Women, to be held March 26–28, 1971, at Harvard.*
- *A demonstration on April 17, 1971, called "Women's Liberation Day" with the following demands: "Free abortion, free, twenty-four-hour, community-controlled child-care centers, equal employment and educational opportunities, repeal of laws governing private sexual behavior." One of the speakers at the rally on the Boston Common was Maryanne Weathers, an early*

member of Female Liberation and the Black and Third World Women's Alliance.

In an article in the first issue of the Second Wave *titled "New England Women's Coalition," Chris Hildebrand wrote:*

> In the first few months since August 26, the New England Women's Coalition has grown from five to seventeen organizations. Some of the groups in the coalition didn't even exist prior to August 26.
>
> Those of us working in the coalition felt a need to give powerful organizational expression to our growing movement. We believe that female oppression is so profound and all-encompassing that it will take the combined energies of every sister to win total liberation.
>
> We do not propose that this coalition take the place of any women's organization.

Delpfine: The New England Congress to Unite Women was a great success. We had eight hundred women from all over the New England region.

Chris: The Harvard conference was phenomenal. Flo Kennedy, the Black civil rights activist, feminist, and lawyer who had written extensively on abortion rights, spoke at the conference. Another speaker was Florence Luscomb, a former suffragist and a lifetime activist in the women's, labor, civil liberties, and peace movements. After the conference, we had a big party at the Charles Street Meeting House. We danced a lot. It was great.

Delpfine: I remember that celebration party at the Charles Street Meeting House. I remember dancing to Aretha Franklin's song "Respect."

Evelyn: Female Liberation had a booth at the April 17 Women's Liberation Day. We sold nearly $200 worth of literature, including about a hundred copies of the *Second Wave.*

Chris: Looking back, it was amazing how much we accomplished and were involved in during the time after August 26, 1970—conferences, demonstrations, planning meetings, regular business meetings, writing and distributing the magazine the *Second Wave,* our weekly Female Liberation newsletter, and more. We expended so much energy every day. We were floating on clouds, so excited about everything we were doing.

Anaïs Nin Meeting

Boden: I had an absolute passion for the diaries of Anaïs Nin.[*] I discovered that Evelyn and Nancy Williamson also shared my passion. Each of us had read all five of them. They had really inspired us about what the possibilities were to be a woman, the different ways you could live. The intimate journal writing was really different for us. We talked about this together, and then we had this idea that we would write to her and tell her that there were these feminists in the United States who absolutely adored

---

[*]   Anaïs Nin, *The Diary of Anaïs Nin* (New York: Harcourt, Brace and Jovanovich, 1966).

her and were inspired by her writing. Nancy was our writer. She was an incredible writer; she wrote poetry, fiction, and a lot of the articles for our journal. She was probably the one who composed the letter.

Anaïs Nin wrote back. We were shocked. She couldn't believe that these feminists in Boston knew about her, let alone were inspired by her. She was very intrigued. We wrote back and forth and invited her to come speak. She agreed and she came. We booked Emerson Hall at Harvard University, but had to move the venue to the Old Cambridge Baptist Church because of the overwhelming number of people who wanted to attend. It was sold out because many people knew and loved her work.

She donated all the proceeds to the *Second Wave*. We did an interview with her. It was just magical. It was a total inspiration.

Evelyn: I read the diaries in 1967 when I was in college at the University of Michigan in Ann Arbor. When I first met Nancy Williamson through Female Liberation, we became close friends. I introduced her to the diaries of Anaïs Nin. Nancy was a writer and had kept her own diary for many years. She was amazed and enchanted with the Anaïs Nin diaries. Nancy wrote to Anaïs on our behalf, and created the groundwork for our lovely relationship with her.

The speaking engagement we sponsored for Anaïs Nin was just like everything else we did in Female Liberation. It went way beyond what we expected. There were people standing outside who could not get in. The whole inside of the church was filled with people. All the pews were taken. There were people sitting and standing in the aisles. We sold 1,100 tickets.

Claudette: Seeing Anaïs Nin in person and later reading her diaries made a huge impression on me. I confess I was a bit scandalized with her candid reveling in her sexuality and her willingness to share the sexual aspects of her many relationships. This was all so contrary to what I had been taught. Sex was supposed to be secret and never spoken about. I thought of her as a very courageous and powerful woman to dare to do this.

Ann Marie: I also attended the meeting for Anaïs Nin. I helped to collect the donations for Female Liberation.

Boden: Subsequent to the meeting we held for Anaïs Nin in Cambridge, there was an artists and writers weekend with Anaïs outside of New York City, in Rye, New York. Anaïs invited Nancy Williamson, who was our writer, and Evelyn to attend. All these amazing artists were there. It was called "a celebration of life." It was a long, four-day weekend. That was an amazing experience for them.

Evelyn: Yes, I was there with Nancy Williamson. Everybody else at the weekend was an artist and had something to offer in that department. I felt a little uncomfortable because I wasn't an artist. Nancy read from her diary. I read some passages from Leon Trotsky on art. It was held at a big, old home—a mansion. It was an incredible setting.

They had a dinner where everybody got together. I had not worn a dress for a couple of years. I was in Female Liberation, and we didn't wear that type of clothing. But they made a point of wearing dresses to the dinner, so I had to borrow one of Nancy's dresses to wear. It was awkward because I didn't have the shoes. You need the whole get-up. But it didn't matter, because everybody was an artist, and everyone was different from each other. It was wonderful.

There were sessions where people talked about art and what they did. One woman made books. It was very relaxing, beautiful, and a wonderful experience. I did not have a personal conversation with Anaïs Nin, but it was great to be with her. It was really nice to see what she created around her. She had a particular type of elegance and honesty. She was an incredible mix of a lot of different things. For me, she brought feminism into the arts. Yet she did not go the direction we went. She was still totally feminine. Her world was more of the emotional realm.

The book *Celebration with Anaïs Nin*, edited by Valerie Harms, documents the weekend retreat.* In that book, I'm quoted as saying:

> I think what you said about the reasons you write diaries instead of novels is true—that people really need the direct experience and need to unmask themselves. I was just going to say that when I read the diary such a direct and honest statement overwhelmed me; it doesn't have any of the constructions of literature. In many ways I was really looking for the diary. I was looking for that kind of openness.

Also in the book, Harms goes on to describe me "as a revo-

---

*   Valerie Harms, ed., *Celebration with Anaïs Nin* (Riverside, CT: Magic Circle Press, 1973).

lutionary inside a dancer, inside a keypunch operator; who said her purple robe for Saturday dinner was the first dress she had worn in two and a half years; who spoke and smiled with the radiance of Consciousness VIII or IX, I couldn't tell which and read Trotsky to the artists on Sunday afternoon."

A group of us—maybe four or five—went to New York City to interview Anaïs Nin for the *Second Wave*. It was a very warm encounter. Our relationship with her was genuinely enriching for us as well as for her. We visited her in her apartment—the living room was a modest size and decorated simply. It was colorful. We gathered around her for the interview—some of us sat on the floor. I remember being there, being in the room with her, although I was not the one designing the interview or asking the questions. Our whole interlude with Anaïs was truly an unexpected gift.

Boden: Evelyn, Nancy Williamson, and I also wrote an article about Anaïs Nin for the *Second Wave* called "A Mirror for Us All." This article first appeared in *Boston After Dark*.

Child-Care Referendum

As part of the Cambridge Child Care Referendum Committee, Female Liberation worked on a referendum that appeared on the Cambridge, Massachusetts, ballot in November 1971. It called for free, community-controlled child care available up to twenty-four hours a day. In order to get the referendum on the ballot, 3,400 valid signatures of registered Cambridge voters were needed. The referendum passed, with 16,500 Cambridge voters showing their support.

A community forum was held June 5 at the First Baptist Church in Cambridge. Female Liberation member Nancy Williamson spoke.. Reporting on the June 5 forum of one hundred people in the Female Liberation newsletter, it says: "Many women began circulating petitions after the forum and have reported an immediate and enthusiastic response from the community. The campaign has also received wide coverage from the Boston and Cambridge papers as well as radio and TV."

Ann Marie: The idea for the child-care referendum came out of the New England Women's Coalition meeting in February 1971 and was then endorsed by the New England Congress to Unite Women in March 1971.

Marnette O'Brien and I worked full time in the office in Cambridge. We had to collect the signatures to get the demand for free, twenty-four-hour, community-controlled child care on the ballot in November, and this was June. We petitioned door-to-door. Everybody was crazy about it, because Cambridge was at that time about 90 percent working class, although there are elite universities there. The referendum was well received. We also had educational materials on the need for public child care, and on the history of public child care during the Depression and during World War II.

After we had enough signatures to get on the ballot, we wrote a brochure explaining free, twenty-four-hour, community-controlled child care. People just loved it.

I came up with the idea for the slogan on our button, "For childcare for all." We also had a big rummage sale. All during the fall, we went door-to-door talking to people. We won 76 percent of the vote. The Cambridge City Council never put up the money for it, though.

Chris: The referendum became our big project that spring and summer. Ann Marie and Marnette were running the referendum campaign in Cambridge.

The idea for doing the referendum in Cambridge gained momentum after the occupation of the building at 888 Memorial Drive in March 1971.* This ten-day occupation of a building owned by Harvard involved hundreds of Boston feminists. They demanded a women's center and low-income housing for the community. Women from the surrounding community came and brought their children, and discussed the need for child care. The women who occupied the building demanded that Harvard provide community child care in the building.

Jeanne: I remember being part of the rummage sale we had for the child-care referendum. We rented a car with a sound machine on top, and I, along with one other person, went up and down Massachusetts Avenue to tell people there was a rummage sale. They never should have put the two of us in the car together. We had quite a thing going with this sound truck. We were having an absolute blast.

We succeeded in getting the referendum on the ballot. However, the wording of the referendum was frightening for some peo-

---

*   The occupation is documented in the movie *Left on Pearl* available from leftonpearl.org.

ple. They thought, "They are going to take my kids twenty-four hours for free!" It wasn't formulated in such a way as to enlist votes from the average citizen.

As the Cambridge City Council continued to stall on implementation of the childcare referendum, Female Liberation, along with the Cambridge Child Care Committee, stepped up the pressure. In July 1972, one hundred and fifty people, including about sixty children, massed in front of Cambridge City Hall. The "Child-in" received extensive press coverage. However, the City Council still continued to stall.

On September 22, 1972, the Cambridge Child Care Committee sent a letter to the City Council of Cambridge. The letter states, "The City Council, through its inaction, has evidently rejected the Ordinance and chosen to ignore the mandate of 16,500 Cambridge voters."

Female Liberation and Gay Liberation

Chris: The first time I saw gay liberation banners was at the August 26, 1970, women's rights demonstration. Diana and others were there with their banners. Afterward, we all went over to the Female Liberation office. Diana and Gale King, another leader of Daughters of Bilitis, started coming to the Monday night Female Liberation meetings. At this time Female Liberation was growing by leaps and bounds.

Diana: Yes, I did start coming to meetings then. It was great. I felt part of a bigger movement. I, along with a few others, had formed the first chapter in Boston of Daughters of Bilitis, a lesbian organization. I wanted to bring along the women I was working with in that group. I felt the need to involve ourselves in other stuff. I was attracted to the idea. It spoke to me.

Chris: Yes, I remember when you came to Female Liberation and we started carrying *The Ladder,* the newspaper of Daughters of Bilitis, in our office. Everyone was excited about hooking up with Daughters of Bilitis.

Nancy: I remember many of us in Female Liberation marched in solidarity with the emerging gay liberation movement. We carried our Female Liberation banners in the June 1971 Gay Pride march and rally in both Boston and New York City. We sold copies of the *Second Wave.*

Boden: I went to the Gay Pride marches in both Boston and New York City. The demonstration I remember the most was the one in New York. I'll never forget marching down Fifth Avenue with my sisters in a sea of gay people. The march was huge. I started to feel the power that we had as a mass movement and felt invincible.

Chapter 5

FEMALE LIBERATION AND THE ANTI-VIETNAM WAR MOVEMENT

During the years 1968 to 1972, the fight against the US war in Vietnam grew into a massive movement that shook the country.

Following the US invasion of Cambodia on April 30, 1970, protests erupted on hundreds of campuses throughout the country. On May 4, Ohio National Guardsmen opened fire on a protest at Kent State University, killing four students. Eleven days later, two students were killed at Jackson State College in Mississippi, a predominately Black college, when police again opened fire on a student demonstration.

In response to the killings of students and to the Cambodia invasion, a national student strike developed, involving millions of college and high school students. This strike had a profound effect on US society as a whole, further deepening antiwar sentiment.

On the weekend of May 23–24, 1970, a conference was held at the Massachusetts Institute of Technology, organized by a planning committee of representatives from a large number of New England anti–Vietnam War groups. This conference was the scene of an event described in this chapter.

Female Liberation activists were part of these mobilizations against the war. Several leaders of Female Liberation spoke at antiwar protests, linking the fight against the war to the struggle for female emancipation.

Ginny: I was involved in the anti–Vietnam War movement while I was a student at Boston University. Through SDS I was involved with other issues as well.

In the fall of 1969, workers at the big Lynn, Massachusetts, General Electric (GE) plant were forced out on strike.* The BU business school invited a GE executive to come speak on campus. SDS decided to organize a protest in solidarity with the strikers.

We didn't have a definite plan. Outside of the ballroom where the speech was being given, we had an open discussion and vote about whether or not to break in and disrupt the event. Someone came running up to the crowd and reported that there were a hundred cops hiding in the Student Union ready to pounce on us. So, in front of the BU dean of students and a Boston police captain, the throng of students voted to immediately and peacefully disband the demonstration.

The police captain had a walkie-talkie with which he could direct his troops. As we left the Student Union building, uniformed and plainclothes cops came rushing out of the cafeteria, library, and off the street swinging batons at every young person in their path. It was a genuine, unprovoked police riot.

---

*   On October 27, 1969, 150,000 GE workers, organized in several unions, began a strike that lasted over three months. The strike won widespread support from students and others.

They beat students and threw twenty-two of us into three paddy wagons that they'd sprayed with tear gas. When we pulled into the police garage in South Boston, a racist enclave, they forced us to walk to cells through a gauntlet of cops who beat us with billy clubs. It was brutal and terrifying.

It was also a blatant violation of our First Amendment rights to free speech and peaceful protest. All twenty-two of us were convicted on a couple of misdemeanors. In addition, three students, including me, were convicted of felonies—assault and battery on a police officer. Talk about standing things on their head!

I deeply regret not suing the cops for brutality and the university administration for complicity. I believe it could have been a huge case with national implications. It might have startled the country into better seeing how students were working for positive changes, while every level of the government, from the president to the army to the FBI to local police forces, were ready to use violence to prevent democratic dissent.

In some way, such a case might have impacted the horrific murders of students the following spring by the Ohio National Guard and Mississippi police.

My junior year ended in 1970 with the nationwide student strike against the war and the Kent State and Jackson State murders. We had shut down BU! And students across the country had shown that we were a force to be reckoned with.

Ann Marie: In 1970, I worked full time in the office of Vietnam '70, a Cambridge-based antiwar coalition that organized a referendum calling for withdrawal of US troops from Vietnam. It was part of a nationwide effort to "let the people vote on war."

Claudette: In May 1970, a mass student assembly was called at Emmanuel College, where I was a student, in response to the killings at Kent State. The dean of students took the stage in a big auditorium on campus and implored us not to vote to shut down the school. It's a testament to the depth of the antiwar movement that the college administration honored our vote—cancelling all classes and deciding not to go ahead with commencement. A number of us stayed around on campus, organizing ourselves to speak about the war at local Catholic high schools.

Chris: In the spring of 1970, all hell broke loose in the antiwar movement and on the campuses. That's when the student strikes in response to the killings at Jackson State and Kent State were happening and the Student Mobilization Committee (SMC) was growing. There was a big conference at MIT in May that was called as an emergency to plan a national response to deepen the student strikes. Several organizations came to break up the meeting, armed with brass knuckles and baseball bats. There was a huge defense that Jeanne, Delpfine, and Pat were part of. The meeting was able to continue.

Ginny: I was a member of SDS at the time of the antiwar conference at MIT. I was totally in favor of standing in solidarity against any form of violence and was for the right of any group to have their meetings. I went over to MIT to help defend SMC's right to hold a conference without being disrupted. Who was there but these tough-looking women in leather boots. They were from Female Liberation. I remember Jeanne Lafferty in particular, because of her wild, red hair. I could never forget her.

Jeanne: I was home at the time the MIT conference started. I was not a part of the conference. I got a call from Harvey, my husband at the time, who said that a group whose aim was to disrupt the meeting was marching into the conference and it was thought they had weapons, not guns, but weapons nonetheless. Delpfine, Pat, and I got called because they thought we were superwomen, since we'd been studying karate.

We were on the mezzanine, where there were four ways to get in. What happened is that they came to where I was standing. We were all jammed in. I knew how to use my fists correctly and put my body behind a punch. Most importantly, I knew to look the person in the eye—because when guys fight, they try to protect their face—and so I hit them. They had brass knuckles and nunchucks, but I was able to put at least seven men out of action. Later that day, when Harvey came home, he said that everyone was talking about what I did.

≈

The April 24, 1971, anti–Vietnam War demonstration in Washington, DC, drew over five hundred thousand people. Leading up to the demonstration, Female Liberation helped to circulate a leaflet about the United Women's Contingent. At a business meeting in March Female Liberation voted to approve a statement that said in part: "We felt that our interests as women against the war could most effectively be shown through marching together. We will join with other forces when it is possible to express ourselves as women against the war."

The May 2, 1971, Female Liberation newsletter reported:

April 24 was the largest display of antiwar sentiment that this country has seen to date with almost a million people marching in the streets of Washington, D.C. and San Francisco demanding immediate and total withdrawal. For the first time women marched as a group, an open display of the power of sisterhood in forcing the U.S. out of S. E. Asia. We carried feminist banners showing the relationship of the war to the oppression of women and chanted slogans demanding that the money spent on Vietnam be used for free 24-hour childcare, free abortion and equal pay. We carried the Female Liberation banner and also sold The Second Wave—*selling about 1,000!*

Boden: I was the office manager of the Greater Boston Peace Action Coalition for the April 24, 1971, anti–Vietnam War demonstration in Washington, DC. That was a job I was very proud of. I worked my tail off. An office manager was the one who wheeled and dealt all the time and made things happen but was not necessarily the one to give the speeches. We organized a large number of buses to go to DC for the rally. There were buses from all over the country. People being visible in the streets really did seem to help end the war. I saw the power of organizing—that you can really make a difference.

I spoke at an antiwar demonstration in the fall of 1971 in Cape Cod, sponsored by a newly formed peace action group. Women planned the entire event. They asked Female Liberation to send a speaker and to help them set up a women's group. I was a nervous wreck. I realized that public speaking was not my forte.

I hated it. I was always in awe of Nancy Williamson and Jeanne Lafferty's speeches. I'm sure my speech was very short.

Evelyn: All of the movements at that time—the women's movement, the civil rights movement, the gay liberation movement—we were all part of the anti–Vietnam War movement. We supported each other. The women's movement had speakers and led workshops at national and regional anti–Vietnam War conferences. Leaders of the women's movement spoke at mass anti–Vietnam War demonstrations. We marched under our own banners. Female Liberation sold incredible amounts of women's literature at these events. We were exposed to people from all over the country who were hungry for this information. It was exciting to stand and be recognized as women together in the public arena, wielding our own power and influence as a group.

≈

On July 2–4, 1971, the National Peace Action Coalition held a conference in New York City to plan for summer and fall actions of the antiwar movement. Female Liberation was one of the forty-three women's groups from all over the country represented at the conference.

The Female Liberation newsletter of July 12, 1971, states: "150 sisters met in the Women and War workshop. We voted to continue to build the United Women's Contingent for the demonstrations. We hope to reach out to as many women as possible to demonstrate against the war." Pat Galligan from Female Liberation gave a speech at the opening session of the conference.

In the fall of 1971, demonstrations continued against the war in

Vietnam. Pat Galligan spoke at the rally in Boston, saying: "American women and the people of Southeast Asia have the same enemy. We want the government out of the war, out of our wombs, and out of our way."

A women's antiwar conference took place in Toronto, April 9–11, 1971. At the conference, five hundred American and Canadian women met with six women from Indochina: two from the National Liberation Front of South Vietnam, two from North Vietnam, and two from Laos.

Chris: In the spring of 1971, the Toronto Women's Conference was held. Vietnamese women came. Female Liberation sent Maryanne Weathers and Hanna Takashige. They came back and gave a report. It was very exciting. They got to meet privately with the Vietnamese women.

Maryanne: I was at the conference and what I remember is that the Vietnamese women gave us each gifts. These were necklaces that had been made out of pieces of US planes that the Vietnamese had shot down!

Chapter 6

THE FIGHT TO LEGALIZE ABORTION

One of the key issues affecting women in the late 1960s and early 1970s was the fact that abortion was illegal. Prior to Roe v. Wade, thousands of women seeking abortions died in back alleys at the hands of butchers. Women began demanding control of their own bodies. Female Liberation believed that the fight for safe, legal, and accessible abortion was central to women's emancipation.

In addition, Female Liberation took up the demand "No forced sterilizations." This was seen as extremely important, since many Puerto Rican women in particular, as well as women from other oppressed nationalities, were sterilized against their will or knowledge.

Evelyn: I wrote the pamphlet, *Knowledge and Control: The Issue of Abortion*, in July of 1970. Jeanne, Boden, and I mimeographed, collated, and stapled hundreds of copies. We worked through the night. We got really giddy after a while and started dancing around to the rhythm of the mimeograph machine spitting out copies. The pamphlet was a compilation of what was out there at the time, which was hardly anything. It was a hidden subject. In the introduction, I wrote, "This pamphlet was compiled to help educate women about the issue of abortion so that they may more actively take part in the movement for free and legal abortion for all women."

Jeanne: Evelyn and I did a number of things together. She wrote a pamphlet on reproductive rights. We had this old, hand-cranked mimeo machine. Evelyn, Boden, and I spent the whole day and night in the office running it off. I remember us coming out of there greeting the morning light, and we were still beating to the rhythm of the machine.

Ginny: In 1971, the issues of abortion and contraception were becoming very important. Contraception was illegal in Massachusetts unless you were married or had some medical reason for it. The laws were very reactionary. It was illegal to display the pill. You had to go to a gynecologist, and either you had to say that you were married or they had to say they would give it to you to regulate your menstrual cycle. That's how we got birth control. This was unacceptable from both a practical and a feminist point of view. Feminists joined with others who were already demanding legalization of contraception and abortion.

I believe it was feminists who posed the issue as a woman's right to choose if and when to become a mother. That was the phrase that was later truncated into the "right to choose."

Diana: I remember doing a lot of work around abortion in the days before *Roe v. Wade*. We were holding demonstrations. We had a meeting at Faneuil Hall in Boston with Barbara Roberts, a doctor who was an outspoken supporter of abortion rights. Those were heavy times.

Nancy: When I joined Female Liberation, I started to get way more serious about making change—effective change. I joined along with my two roommates at the time. Together we had come to the conclusion that something had to be done around the issue of abortion. This was the number-one issue for women. Women were dying from back-alley abortions, and we had to do something. Female Liberation was the perfect place to get something going around this issue because it was an action-oriented organization.

Maryanne: I wrote an article, "Black Women and Abortion," in March of 1971. At that time, I was a member of the Black and Third World Women's Alliance as well as Female Liberation. Later, in the summer of 1971, we published the article in the second issue of Female Liberation's magazine, the *Second Wave.*

≈

Twelve Female Liberation members were among the two hundred in attendance at a meeting held June 12, 1971, in New York City, to plan the National Women's Abortion Conference. The ad-hoc Abortion Conference Committee issued a letter dated June 24, 1971, seeking endorsements of the conference. The letter was signed by a broad range of women, including Nancy Williamson from Female Liberation, Maryanne Weathers from Female Liberation and the Black and Third World Women's Liberation Alliance, Mary Daly, an assistant professor of theology at Boston College, and others.

Nancy Rosenstock and Evelyn Clark went to work in New York for three weeks to help organize the conference.

The conference held in New York City in July of 1971 founded the Women's National Abortion Action Coalition (WONAAC). Over one thousand women from all over the country participated. Female Liberation sent thirty-six women, the largest representation from any single women's group. The conference came out of a call from women in New Haven, Connecticut, who were proposing a united nationwide campaign for the repeal of all abortion laws and an end to forced sterilization.

Nancy: Female Liberation issued a position paper for the conference. It said in part: "As feminists we believe that a campaign to repeal all abortion laws is a vital part of our struggle for the total liberation of our sex."

Delpfine: I remember the July WONAAC conference well because I chaired the plenary sessions. The conference adopted a plan for abortion law repeal that included mass demonstrations, abortion hearings, testimonials, caravans, speak-outs, and class-action lawsuits. "No forced sterilizations" and "Repeal of all contraceptive laws" were also adopted as demands. The conference called for demonstrations to take place in November 1971.

Nancy: In August 1971, the Boston Women's Abortion Coalition (BOWAAC) held its founding meeting. I gave a report to this meeting on the July WONAAC conference. Ending that report, I said, "Our sisters in the first wave of feminism won the right to vote; so now we will win the right to abortion, one of the first steps in our fight for complete liberation."

After I graduated from Boston University in 1971, I moved to New York City and was on the national staff of WONAAC. We had an office on 14th Street.

In September 1971, I moved to Washington, DC, for three months to help organize and build for the November demonstration. The demonstration ended up being much smaller than we had expected, with 1,200 in attendance.

Chris: I went to Washington, DC, early to help build for the November 1971 demonstration, along with some other women in Female Liberation. Unfortunately, a massive effort was under way accusing the organizers of being communists. This red-baiting campaign was aimed at frightening away potential marchers. The media and scheduled speakers, including Shirley Chisholm and Billie Jean King, received news releases on WONAAC letterhead by a supposed disgruntled staff member claiming that the demonstration was a communist front. Shirley Chisholm and Billie Jean King withdrew their participation. I remember that Maryanne called Shirley Chisholm on the phone and blasted her for this, for selling out to the FBI. Years later it was revealed through freedom of information documents that the letter on WONAAC stationery and the entire campaign was carried out by FBI agents as part of COINTELPRO—a covert counterintelligence program aimed at disrupting, sabotaging, surveilling, and infiltrating domestic political organizations. FBI agents were active in the women's movement, attempting to disrupt its growth and success.

Nancy: The abortion law repeal campaign was an international effort. When I was on WONAAC's staff, I wrote a letter to a women's group in Nottingham, England, that was organizing to have a tour of a women's rights activist from the United States. In the letter I said, "We are calling on all women all over the world to unite in international solidarity to show our strength and power and to build the kind of movement that truly can put an end to the brutalization and mutilation of our sisters."

≈

The second national conference of WONAAC was held at Boston University in February 1972 and was attended by 1,300 people.

Ginny: The focus of Boston University Female Liberation was to organize a national conference about reproductive choice and get official sponsorship for it.

We went to a student council meeting where we wheeled in a reel-to-reel projector. We said, We're going to ask you for money to help us put on a national educational organizing conference for women's right to choose abortion and for safe, legal birth control available to all. We want you to watch this short movie, which will explain why. We turned on the movie, which had been made in Cambridge. I forget the name of the movie. It was a movie about illegal abortions and what happens to women when they get these—how their insides were ripped open and others bled to death. Some women survived, but were never able to have children. The movie showed the terrible, terrible things that were happening with back-alley abortions. It was a very powerful movie.

When the lights went on, we proposed that they give us all the facilities for free and—I forget what the budget was—$1,000, or something like that, to help with national publicity. They agreed to do it. The student government of BU hosted the conference.

Later, I was invited to come on the WONAAC staff to help with fundraising. I moved to New York City in December 1972 to be on staff.

Dany: In 1972, I was the office manager of Female Liberation. We put out the weekly newsletter, as well as the *Second Wave*. We had quite a large mailing list, over a thousand women. We had weekly meetings, but they were dwindling in size. We used to have parties to put out the newsletters. It was a big deal putting it out—mimeographing, collating, putting labels on. It was the better part of a night involving fifteen people. But even that had gotten to the point where it was two or three people at the most doing anything.

BOWAAC was doing work on abortion, and their office was literally down the hall from Female Liberation in the building in Central Square, Cambridge. We were neighbors. You could watch women walking up the stairs past the Female Liberation office and going directly to BOWAAC. At that point, Female Liberation wasn't doing much of anything.

There was going to be a rally on the Boston Common demanding safe, legal abortion. Female Liberation was involved but was not the key organization. If members of Female Liberation wanted to get involved, they just went straight to the BOWAAC office.

Ann Marie: From the end of 1972 until the *Roe v. Wade* decision in 1973, I was the office manager of BOWAAC.

Diana: In May 1972, I spoke at a rally as part of Abortion Action Week called by WONAAC that was held throughout the country to continue efforts to legalize abortion. I said:

> Here is one way in which gay women relate to the abortion movement—and this has to do with the word "control." Control of our bodies and our sexual lives has been taken away from us and given to the state, and here in Massachusetts to the Catholic Church. And the reason behind this control is to perpetuate the myth of women's role as wife and mother, something we as gay women have been fighting against for years. The same people who make anti-homosexual laws also make anti-abortion laws. We must all join together to fight these laws, and we must fight them with the anger and the assertion that it's NOT the church, it's NOT the state's . . . or anyone else's but A WOMAN'S RIGHT TO CHOOSE!!!

Ginny: In January of 1973, the Supreme Court announced the *Roe v. Wade* decision legalizing abortion up to the 24th week. We had won! We had helped to change and vastly improve women's lives forever, or so it seemed.

Chris: We won the right to legal abortion with the victory of *Roe v. Wade.* In addition, the ERA began to be ratified in state after state. It appeared that women would finally be included in the US Constitution. Affirmative action consent decrees were signed in major industries. Women were entering nontraditional jobs, which gave us more economic independence.

Ginny: At the same time, troops were being withdrawn from Vietnam. It felt like the youth radicalization had accomplished historic victories. It was a happy time. Some of us thought that progress for human rights and liberation might continue forward step by step, and we might even see a new American Revolution in our lifetime.

Chapter 7

DRAWING BROADER CONCLUSIONS: FEMINISM AND SOCIALISM

As a result of being active in the women's liberation movement, some members of Female Liberation began to draw broader conclusions about what was needed to win complete emancipation for women. A number began to study Marxism and socialism.

At a time when most socialist groups were hesitant to fully embrace women's liberation, some women were attracted to the Young Socialist Alliance (YSA) and Socialist Workers Party (SWP)*, which were then playing a key role in the anti–Vietnam War movement and were early and enthusiastic supporters of the women's liberation movement. Some members of Female Liberation made the decision to join these socialist groups; many did not.

The issue of socialism has arisen in some assessments of Female Liberation. Several books about the second wave of feminism repeat a falsehood that Cell 16 and Female Liberation were "taken over by the SWP/

---

* The Young Socialist Alliance (YSA) was the youth group of the Socialist Workers Party (SWP).

YSA." Alice Echols, in her book, Daring to Be Bad: Radical Feminism in America 1967–1975, *states: "Two of the original members of Cell 16 became involved in the SWP while still involved in the group. A schism arose. The non-SWP women circulated a letter throughout the movement alerting women to the SWP's efforts to 'infiltrate' feminist groups." Flora Davis, in her book,* Moving the Mountain: The Women's Movement in America since 1960, *continues along the same lines. In a chapter titled "Attacks from the Left," she states: "Between 1970 and 1972, the Socialist Workers Party made a number of attempts to take over women's centers, women's unions, and feminist groups. In the fall of 1970, the SWP succeeded with Boston's Cell 16."*

Through previous chapters in this book, readers have seen that divisions within Female Liberation were rooted in differing perspectives on how to build an effective women's liberation movement. Some of Cell 16's members began to question the small-group approach to the fight for women's liberation—that the movement should be led and organized by small cells of committed women. They instead wanted to build an organization open to all with a mass-action perspective. These differences led to the departure of a handful of the former leaders of the group, who opposed the democratic wishes of the majority of the organization

A number of Female Liberation members drew the conclusions on their own that they needed to be part of the socialist movement. It was only after they joined that the YSA or SWP as organizations decided to participate in building Female Liberation; it was not the other way around.

While none of the women interviewed for this book remain members or supporters of the SWP today, readers will find their comments on the ties between feminism and socialism of interest.

Delpfine: In 1969, my initial radicalization was around women's liberation. The anti–Vietnam War movement was going on at the time, but I wasn't involved in antiwar activities. Later, as I sold the journal *No More Fun and Games* in Harvard Square next to Black Panther Party members selling their paper, I became more aware of the concurrent movements—female liberation, Black liberation, and antiwar. I didn't know how it was all going to come together, but I knew it had to. I started to think about the need for something that could unite us all. I shared a house in Somerville where we had Marxist study groups. Socialism began to make sense to me. I attended a series of talks by Peter Camejo, a leader of the SWP. That led me to join the YSA in May 1970.

Nancy: I was involved in the antiwar movement at Boston University and was a member of SDS. In addition, I had been around various socialist organizations. From 1970 to 1971, I shared an apartment with two other women in Central Square, Cambridge, a few blocks from the new Female Liberation office. My roommates and I were very active in Female Liberation. We began to get way more serious about wanting to make effective change. The three of us started checking out different socialist organizations. We would each go to a different meeting on a given night and report to each other.

We started looking for answers. For a while, I subscribed to the theory of the "Fourth World Manifesto."* The idea was that women were the fourth world and we could make a revolution without men.

---

* "The Fourth World Manifesto" was written by Barbara Burris in 1971.

The different socialist organizations that we initially took a look at did not support women's liberation. Then I went to a talk that Peter Camejo gave at BU on the Cuban Revolution and was positively blown away. The other socialist groups that we had checked out did not support the Cuban Revolution. Chris and Ginny were in Female Liberation as well as the YSA and SWP. I started attending Militant Labor Forums at the SWP headquarters. Chris would pick me up on Friday nights and basically drag me to the forums. My roommates and I would sit in the front row. We were very provocative. We had to be convinced. We had not worked with men for a year and a half, and we had to be positively sure that this socialist organization supported women's liberation. After moving to New York City in the summer of 1971, I joined the YSA and a few months later the SWP.

Boden: After meeting and talking with some of the women in Female Liberation who were also in the YSA, I started attending forums and eventually joined. I wanted to expand my political horizons and work in the antiwar movement. Becoming a socialist was a logical step to keep growing politically. I think early on we had a reading club. I just ate up those books. One book in particular that I remember was *Fanshen,* by William Hinton, which describes the land reform campaign in China during the late 1940s and the oppression of women at that time in China.

Learning about different cultures and political struggles around the world was fascinating to me. It was all the stuff you didn't learn in school—about the labor movement in the United States and what happened in all the revolutions around the world. I just gobbled it up. I was in Ann Arbor at the University of Michigan when Martin Luther King was killed. The campus came to a standstill. I started reading books about the oppression of African Americans, such as Black Panther Party (BPP) writings and books by BPP leader Eldridge Cleaver. I couldn't get enough of it. It was like, "Oh, there is a whole world out there."

Chris: I was a member of the SWP and in the fall of 1970, after participating in the August 26 women's march, I joined Female Liberation. Four of the members of Female Liberation—Jeanne, Delpfine, Pat Galligan, and Evelyn—had joined the socialist movement in the spring and summer of 1970. They were four absolutely outstanding, feminists. They were true leaders. They always knew exactly what to do next.

The SWP and YSA never "intervened" in or "entered" Female Liberation. The women from Female Liberation who joined the YSA in 1970 taught us about feminism and changed the organization for the better, that's for sure. Our outlook for what the women's movement needed to do to move forward converged with theirs, partially because of their leadership and direction.

Evelyn: One of the things that attracted me to the YSA, especially since I had been studying Tae Kwon Do was the discipline of the organization. In Female Liberation, we made a lot of mistakes, and we were inexperienced organizationally, but we were always serious. We were never playing games. When I understood how the YSA worked—the seriousness and commitment involved—I really liked it.

In 1973 when the Supreme Court decision *Roe v. Wade,* legalizing abortion, was passed, whatever mantle that I had taken on when I began my political journey four and a half years earlier dropped away, as well as my desire and need to be in that arena. I eventually left the SWP and my formal political life.

My study of socialism and Marxism showed me how the world worked. My study of feminism showed me my place in it. The organizational skills and ideas I was exposed to in the SWP were invaluable, and I am grateful that I was allowed to experience how they operated and benefited the mass movements of that time.

Claudette: I was a student at Emmanuel College and was involved in the anti–Vietnam War movement. After graduating and as a result of this activity, I became acquainted with the YSA and SWP. These socialist groups were instrumental in organizing many major demonstrations against the Vietnam War. I liked all the movement activities that they were involved in. I was impressed with their enthusiastic embrace of the aspirations of the women's liberation movement. The YSA and SWP had jumped into organizing and supporting the August 1970 women's rights demonstrations. I identified with the approach of building a broad and powerful women's movement. The YSA and SWP were also the first socialist organizations to support the ERA.

I remember attending a socialist education conference sponsored by the YSA and SWP in the summer of 1970. It was so much fun. I was at a self-defense workshop sitting in the back of the room. There were a couple of rows of people on the floor in the front because the room was full. There was some open space in the front. Jeanne came out. She was the emcee. She announced that they were going to need some more space and asked if people would please move back. Nobody paid any attention. She left the room and then Jeanne, Delpfine, and Pat came in. With the first kick, the whole room moved back! It was great.

Ginny: In August of 1970, I left Boston to go to Saskatchewan, Canada, for my last year of college. I went with two male friends. We wanted to study labor history and Marxism. My arrest and conviction for a felony—assault and battery on a police officer—had convinced me that I better know for sure what I stood for and what strategy and tactics I was prepared to engage in before I found myself in another very dangerous situation.

When I returned to Boston in May of 1971, I was a more committed feminist and a stronger socialist as well. I joined the YSA, and, later in 1972, I traveled all over New England giving talks on the Vietnam War, how socialists viewed it, and what socialism was.

I believed that through struggle people could reshape society based on mutual self-interest and mutual respect, which could never develop under a system propelled by a drive for profit and exploitation of humanity and the natural world, i.e., capitalism.

My feminism enriched my passion to be part of a movement to liberate people from the ravages of war, racism, and stupefying ideologies. This feminist wasn't just fighting *against* things and for *other* people anymore. I was also fighting for myself and for a beautiful vision of a better world that would be strongly influenced by feminists, and then improved upon by future generations uninfected by decades of sexist inculcation.

Jeanne: I had been studying Marxism in 1970 and was very interested in it as a tool of analysis. From this study, I developed an understanding and learned from our history that we don't drop our struggle for anything. I started attending classes on socialism sponsored by the YSA. The classes helped me understand why feminism is a revolutionary force in society.

In the spring of 1970, I started attending Militant Labor Forums at the SWP headquarters. Peter Camejo was giving a series of talks on "How to Make a Revolution in the US." I was totally mesmerized. I was hooked because it helped me see a way forward.

I thought about the Black liberation struggle, and I thought Black people are not all going to join Female Liberation to work toward a revolution, and neither are all women going to join the Black Panther Party. We had to build something qualitatively different from all these particular independent movements. We had to build a unified revolutionary organization that fights the source of all the different forms of oppression and for the complete transformation of this system.

Chapter 8

FEMALE LIBERATION SHAPED OUR LIVES

The years we were members of Female Liberation laid the basis for who we are today and what we have done with the rest of our lives. We traveled on different paths after Female Liberation, but continued in our beliefs about the absolute necessity of the fight for women's rights.

Diana: I live in Charlotte, North Carolina. My partner of twenty-five years and I got married after the US Court of Appeals for the Fourth Circuit, which includes North Carolina, ruled in favor of same-sex marriage in 2014. It was wonderful. The North Carolina Republicans carried out a huge campaign for Amendment 1, which aimed to change the state constitution to prohibit the recognition of same-sex marriage. We worked hard to defeat their efforts. The amendment passed a public vote in 2012, but was then ruled unconstitutional in 2014. We were in the friends-of-the-court brief for Marriage Equality USA that went before the Supreme Court in 2015.

I have served on the Board of Directors of the Charlotte chapter of the American Civil Liberties Union. I am also a cofounder and board member of the Reproductive Rights Coalition.

I spend a lot of time at one of the clinics in Charlotte that is under attack.

What I learned from my days in Female Liberation and later in the Boston Women's Abortion Action Coalition have stayed with me and help me today.

Boden: Working in the feminist and antiwar movements in Boston informed my priorities for the rest of my life. I moved to Washington, DC, in 1972. I started going to the Women's Center on R St. NW to hear a new music, which became known as women's music. That's when I really started to find my niche. I went to the farewell concert of the newly formed Olivia collective at George Washington University. I saw a woman, Judy Dlugacz, on the stage mixing the sound. I knew that was what I wanted to do. She referred me to one of the singers that night, Casse Culver, who taught me the rudiments of being a sound mix engineer. I fell in love with her that night, as her lesbian-identified songs mesmerized me. She became my spouse. As a live mix engineer, you are immersed in the sound—it's like being a conductor. As a musician—I had played the French horn—I was in heaven.

Casse and I started Woman Sound together. It was one of the first all-woman sound companies. The whole logic around starting Woman Sound was to not only be able to create clear, musically mixed sound for women, but for everyone fighting for political and social justice. Woman Sound became the sound company in the DC area for most political movement events—it was good and inexpensive. In a letter congratulating Woman Sound for our work at a National Organization for Women rally held at the Capitol at which she spoke in 1976, Gloria Steinem wrote, "Allowing women to hear each other is the basis of this revolution and you are doing that, spiritually as well as technically.*

Later it became my own company, which eventually I renamed City Sound Productions, as many of the events we did were part of the fabric of the city.

When I decided to pursue my dream of becoming a sound engineer and creating a women's sound company, I knew it was the only way I could grow as a woman, as well as stay committed to my politics. I did not do this in a vacuum. The Olivia collective sprung from The Furies. At the time, they were publishing a newsletter, *The Furies*, and developed a political philosophy of lesbian separatism. Many lesbian-owned businesses were springing up all over DC, empowering lesbians.

The launching of Woman Sound was part of a developing Women's Music Cultural Network and coincided with the beginnings of women's music festivals. I mixed sound at the major women's music festivals, including the Michigan Womyn's Music Festival from 1976 to 1987. Woman Sound also did the technical production for many major events—every LGTBQ rights rally on the Mall in Washington, DC, from 1975 to 1993 and all events for NOW. One of the events that I was most proud of was the 1993 March on Washington for Lesbian, Gay and Bi Equal Rights and Liberation. I helped design a delay system (both sound and video) that ensured that over one million people could hear and see on the Washington Mall.*

I sold City Sound Productions in 1988 and decided to pursue

---

*   The national march for lesbian, gay and bi equal rights and liberation was held April 25, 1993. Some five hundred thousand people participated.

a PhD in ethnomusicology at the University of Maryland, where I could combine my interest of music in social movements, world music, and teaching. I co-produced a documentary, *Radical Harmonies,* directed and produced by my best friend, Dee Mosbacher—a history of the Women's Music Network that was released in 2002.*

I became a lecturer at the University of Maryland. I taught classes on such topics as Women's Music and the significance of music in the fight for civil rights, against the military coup in Chile, the South African anti-apartheid struggle, and the events surrounding Tiananmen Square in China.

I was able to teach what I had learned through my participation in Female Liberation and the political movements in which I had been involved. I developed a seminar, "The Power of Musical Performance in Social Engagement," in which students had the opportunity to attend performances that we studied in class. Many of the artists I had known through my work in Woman Sound would come to our class. Being able to share these artists and their musical stories was very meaningful to me and to my students. Together we were able to demonstrate to a whole new generation that when we work together with action and music, we can change the world. I felt my life had come full circle!

Maryanne: I moved to San Francisco in 1972. I did a lot of work for the Women's Building, a women-led community space that advocates self-determination, gender equality, and social justice. I met women there, and we put together the Women's Jail Proj-

---

*   *Radical Harmonies* directed by Dee Mosbacher (2002), available from womanvision.org.

ect. That kind of put us on the map. I got an entry into jail to talk to these women. I was the link between the project and the women in jail.

After the Women's Jail Project, I got involved with Household Workers Rights. My mother was a maid. I was never embarrassed or upset about it. I just didn't understand why they never got any credit. We put out a newsletter and answered complaints of maids and service workers. When we didn't get a decent answer, we would go and picket. That was in the late '70s and early '80s.

Evelyn: The women's movement and my experiences in Female Liberation gave context to my life. It gave me another point of reference for all of my experiences—a broader and deeper view. It relieved a lot of pressure and expectations held as a result of my conditioning. I felt freer, with more choices.

The work that I had done in Female Liberation gave me the confidence and know-how to own and operate a successful massage therapy center in downtown Boston for seventeen years.

The women's movement brought comfort into all of our lives by relaxing and neutralizing the dress codes for everyone. I grew up in a world where a woman was required to wear dresses, nylons, and heels at work and most places. There are many factors that influenced the changes in dress for women and men but the women's movement paved the way.

My work in Female Liberation allowed me to experience an awakening—an elevation in consciousness. I witnessed a mass awakening around me. I have lived long enough now to see how that has been manifested through time and has influenced and affected so many people and behaviors for the better.

My work in Female Liberation gave me lifelong friends who I hold in my heart and one in particular, Jeanne Lafferty, who I have been lucky enough to have in my life. I also have a wealth of memorable experiences.

I don't know why I was in the epicenter at the inception of this movement, but I was, and I am glad of it.

Where are we now? I applaud the Me Too movement, which has continued the consciousness-raising work of feminism, allowing women the confidence to come forward and speak the truth about their lives. I am excited and gratified to see so many women in the public arena in all aspects of life. I have faith in the power of truth and the power of feminism. And I look forward to the continued emergence of more conscious, feminist leaders who will unite all people to bring about the collective change needed in our world today.

Ann Marie: Since Female Liberation, I have continued to work for women's causes such as defending abortion clinics from attacks.

After I got my license as a clinical laboratory technologist, I worked at UCLA, where I was a union steward for Service Employees International Union (SEIU) Local 660.

I was part of a protest of a "right-to-life" meeting in Anaheim in 1981. I also got involved in the lesbian movement in 1980–81. I helped to distribute the newspaper *Lesbian News* in the Los Angeles valley.

As a member of Lavender Left, I was part of the Los Angeles steering committee of the groups that organized people to go to the Second National March on Washington for Lesbian and Gay

Rights in 1987. This march highlighted the plight of the AIDS epidemic and incorporated acts of civil disobedience.

We heard about ACT UP (Aids Coalition to Unleash Power) in New York City. So I, along with a man who was part of Lavender Left—we were probably the most political ones—started an ACT UP chapter in Los Angeles. I wanted to have more of a mass approach, but he went along with the traditional ACT UP stuff—guerrilla activities, etc.

I was treasurer of the Committee for Justice and against Police Brutality in 1991, following the brutal police beating of Rodney King.*

I now live in northern New Jersey. In 1993 I read a book, *A Return to Love* by Marianne Williamson. This led me to become a student of *A Course in Miracles*, a psychological spiritual path to inner peace, which is my way of life today. I continue to participate in antiwar, abortion rights, anti-Trump, and gun-control rallies in my local area.

Chris: The years 1968–1972 were the most amazing time of my life. Getting to spend so much of that time in Boston and as a member of Female Liberation was so exciting. Feminism became a major focus of my political life. Besides the sisterhood, I was also inspired by the world revolution that was happening—Prague,

---

* In March 1991, a number of Los Angeles police officers were videotaped brutally beating Black worker Rodney King. Charged in federal court with violating King's civil rights, the cops were acquitted by an all-white jury in April 1992. In response, riots exploded across Los Angeles, lasting for four days. Fifty-eight people were killed, more than 80 percent of them Black or Latinx, with 17,000 arrested.

Paris, Latin America, Vietnam. The people were rising up. In the United States, we were a part of this. Millions were mobilizing against the war in Vietnam. Young men were resisting the draft. Black, Chicano, and gay people were forming new radical organizations and fighting for their liberation. Women were a part of all of this. But we were fighting for our own liberation from archaic laws and customs that had held us back. Female Liberation was in the forefront, or so it seemed to us.

We were winning—the war in Vietnam was ending and the troops came home. The Vietnamese revolution was victorious after decades of sacrifice and war. The mass mobilizations around the world and in the United States, eventually joined by GIs themselves, were so important and showed the way forward.

After leaving Boston in 1972, I went to San Francisco for a couple of years and then moved to Los Angeles. I was active in various organizations after my time in Boston, including the Coalition of Labor Union Women (CLUW) and the National Organization for Women. Though we worked on important issues, none of these were nearly as personally gratifying to me as my time in Female Liberation.

In both San Francisco and Los Angeles, I worked as a telephone operator for Pacific Telephone. All operators were members of an independent union of ten thousand telephone operators in California. We merged with the Communication Workers of America (CWA). I was active in the campaign to join up with the CWA. In Los Angeles, I was part of the founding of CLUW in 1974.

I was active in CLUW for a number of years. I think the participation of radical feminists and strong union supporters really helped the women leaders of CLUW, who were part of the labor bureaucracy but who were second-class citizens there. It gave them support for helping to change some of the labor movement's positions. For example, the AFL-CIO had been opposed to the Equal Rights Amendment because they claimed it would invalidate protective laws for women. We combated that concept by pointing out that the ERA could extend true protective laws to men and would remove outdated laws such as one that excluded women from working at night. CLUW convinced the AFL-CIO to change its former opposition and to be in favor of the ERA during the time of the "extension,"* helping to organize demonstrations in Illinois and Virginia that I participated in.

When I came back to New Jersey in the winter of 1977–78, I immediately got active in NOW. There was a chapter close to where I was living. We were part of building the big demonstration for the ERA in July 1978 in Washington, DC. Hundreds of thousands were mobilized demanding that Congress pass the extension of time to win three more states.†

Through my union and CLUW, we also organized to support the labor movement in Virginia, which had called a demonstration for the ERA. Through our work, a whole bunch of people from the telephone company went there with our hard hats and our banners. We got our union, the International Brotherhood of

---

*   By 1977, thirty-five states had ratified the constitutional amendment, but Congress had set a deadline of March 22, 1979, to reach the thirty-eight-state threshold the measure needed to pass. Congress later voted to extend the deadline.

†   The national march for the ERA that took place on July 9, 1978, brought out over one hundred thousand people.

Electrical Workers, to support us, and then when we came back we showed them a slide show of all the unions that had been participating.

I retired from Verizon in 2003. When I first got a job with Pacific Telephone in San Francisco in 1972, I had applied to be an installer or another craft job. They told me that there was nothing in my background to show that I could do that type of work. So the only thing I could apply for was to be an operator. They really wanted women to come in and be operators for their entire lives. This was definite discrimination against me.

In 1973, six months after I started, the company was forced to adopt a consent decree that put into place an affirmative action program. AT&T had to go before the government because they were denying women and minorities a lot of the better-paying jobs. It took me a very long time—it actually was when I got back to New Jersey—to get a really good job as a technician. I was an outside installer and then an inside technician before I got into the more advanced technical stuff. They sent us to school, which they had to do once the consent decree passed. But once this decree expired in 1983, they didn't have to send us to school anymore.

In 2006, my sister Ginny and I started a campaign to save a camp that we had gone to as kids. It was a girl's camp in the Adirondacks called Eagle Island. The Girl Scouts owned it, but were getting ready to shut it down. This camp on an island is a National Historic Landmark.

A lot of the things I had learned to do in the women's movement became very useful. We found all of our camp friends from decades ago and got them involved. We had picket lines constantly at the board meetings of the Girl Scouts. We leafleted. We wrote up the history. We did a timeline. We even filed a lawsuit trying to get them to reopen the camp. Finally, a wealthy, anonymous person stepped forward and bought the camp for us. Since then, we have been working hard to bring the camp back to life. In the summer of 2019, we had a soft opening for a few weeks.

It's amazing all the women we have found that have all kinds of skills—carpenters, electricians, etc. We have also hired professional contractors. We have had to raise money—another thing we learned from our movement. We also learned how to inspire people and how to start a newsletter. We have a quarterly newsletter. We have a democratic board. So everything I learned in the women's movement and other social movements, I am still using to this very day. This is not to say that there are not many others leading this effort, but Female Liberation set an example for me of how to fight and win.

Delpfine: After the first WONAAC conference in 1971, I worked in the YSA National Office in New York City to help build the women's movement. I traveled around the country giving speeches about feminism and socialism.

From 1975 to 1983 I lived in Milwaukee, where I was involved in a variety of political activities. One memory I have is of debating a prominent antiabortion activist in front of a large audience in the ballroom of the student union at the University of Wisconsin–Milwaukee. I later was involved in another organized debate, this time over the ERA. While working in a clerical job at UW–Milwaukee, I helped lead a successful campaign to organize state clerical workers into the American Federation of State,

County and Municipal Employees (AFSCME). I later organized the campus picketing when the AFSCME state employees went on strike. I also was active in NOW. At the same time, I was taking classes at UW–Milwaukee to complete my bachelor's degree.

From 1983 to 1991, I was a graduate student at Virginia Tech where I got a PhD in geology. While in graduate school, I traveled to Washington, DC, several times to march for a woman's right to choose.

Since 1993 I have lived in Austin, Texas. It was amazing to be part of the huge January 2017 Women's March in Austin. I retired in 2018 from my job as a technical writer at a software company where I worked for almost twenty-five years.

I cannot imagine what my life would have been like if I had not embraced feminism and Female Liberation. I believe that our activities have made life better for the young women of today. Now it's their turn to take up the fight!

Jeanne: I live in Portland, Maine. After my years in Female Liberation, I not only became a union organizer but also an artist—drawing and painting.

From my days in the women's liberation movement, I learned a lot about organizing—connecting with people. I was able to use that knowledge later when I was a union organizer for AFSCME at Harvard and then at UMass Medical School. While living in Worcester, Massachusetts, I was the organizer of our union local at the medical center. I was on the floor every single day. I knew every single one of the 550 people in the local.

When I went to work at the school of public health at Harvard, a woman approached me and said, "I remember you because you and other women came to Goddard College when I was a student there. You did a karate demonstration. We were never the same after that."

Female Liberation did a lot of good things. What we did made a difference. I just hope there comes a time where a generation of young women can experience something like what we experienced.

Claudette: In 1971, I moved to Oakland, California, where I continued my activities in defense of women's rights. I participated in the August 26, 1972, Women's Rights Day celebration at San Francisco State University. Beginning in 1975, I became active in NOW. I argued for national mass actions for the ERA. I became the chair of the reproductive rights committee of the Oakland/ Berkeley NOW chapter and a board member.

The San Francisco Pro-Choice Coalition formed in response to attacks on abortion rights. I represented my NOW chapter at the coalition meetings. Our chapter was the most radical in the Bay Area and played a key role in helping to maintain the coalition. We held many emergency picket lines at the SF Federal Building. When Operation Rescue stormed a Planned Parenthood clinic in Oakland, NOW along with other organizations mobilized primarily women clinic defenders to escort women into the clinic.*

When Operation Rescue announced that San Jose would be its next target for an entire week of clinic blockades, we moved

---

* Operation Rescue is an antiabortion organization founded in 1986. In the early 1990s, it led several prominent attempts to blockade abortion clinics, most notably in Wichita, Kansas.

into high gear. We organized a massive, sophisticated operation at all the clinics. I was at the largest Planned Parenthood clinic with a walkie-talkie, leading a line of approximately fifty trained clinic volunteers from Planned Parenthood. Across the street, we could see some tall, white males in suits casing us out. We heard that Planned Parenthood was planning to open the lines if Operation Rescue tried to cross. So I went from woman to woman and asked them what they thought. To a woman they said, "We didn't get up at 4:00 a.m. to let them through," and linked arms. Operation Rescue drove away! Later that day, we sent reinforcements to the only clinic they dared to try to break through. By the end of the day, we had defeated Operation Rescue! We had kept the clinics open.

In 1992, I was invited to the Philippines by one of the socialist organizations in that country. They were eager to learn from other socialists about our successful struggles for reproductive rights in the United States. I learned from them that in the Philippines divorce wasn't allowed, birth control was largely unavailable, and abortion was illegal and dangerous. I met women as young as thirteen who had been hired first as bar maids and then became prostitutes. I was also introduced to an organization that helped pregnant women who had been refused care unless they agreed to put their children up for overseas Catholic adoption.

NOW was a powerful and vibrant organization for more than three decades. I enjoyed participating at state and national conferences—lively events with fierce debates and votes on national priorities. My chapter was instrumental in getting NOW to endorse a California single-payer initiative. In 1996, I was active in the effort to defeat Proposition 209, the California initiative to end affirmative action. To assist in that fight, NOW called for an unprecedented nationally focused demonstration in San Francisco, Fight the Radical Right, which drew over thirty thousand people.

I took a job in 1995 at the University of California–Berkeley, where I joined several socialists in launching an independent, statewide union for clerical employees. It was exciting, challenging, and overwhelming to build this union essentially from scratch. I held many different leadership positions. We successfully encouraged members to come forward with issues and strategies against sexist dress codes; sexual, racist, and discriminatory harassment; and the general impotent feeling that the primarily female workforce had experienced. A year-long preparation for a strike in 2002 drew the participation and support of several other unions. Television coverage of our militant rallies electrified our members across the state.

Over time, our independent union became battle-worn against a powerful university administration. Our union eventually affiliated with the Teamsters. Another member and I unsuccessfully sued the Teamsters to overturn the corrupt election. I joined Teamsters for a Democratic Union and was elected to the international steering committee. As a delegate to the 2011 international Teamster convention, I seconded the nomination of the first female candidate for international president.

I marched with hundreds of thousands of others at NOW's broadly sponsored national rallies for women's lives in Washington, DC, in 1995 and 2004. In January 2017, I participated in the national Women's March in Washington, DC. It was truly an amazing action.

That same year, along with thousands, I joined the transformed Democratic Socialists of America.

Although the marches in 2019 were smaller, I was very happy to participate in the Women's March in Oakland and to see the prominent number of Black people in the march.

I have also been involved in opposing US wars in the Middle East and in local environmental fights.

I am grateful to this day for the opportunity through Female Liberation to become part of the sisterhood that informed me and helped me to fight for my rights.

Ginny: I live in Pittsburgh and work as a dog groomer. The newfound self-respect and respect for women that I gained in the early days of the women's movement opened my heart to lesbian love. I have been with my partner for thirty-eight happy years.

I have remained an activist against wars, for reproductive rights, for Black Lives Matter, for civil liberties, and much more. During my time in Pittsburgh, I initiated an unsuccessful class-action lawsuit against a large government contractor who refused to hire women. I have carried my feminism and socialism into several nontraditional jobs: coal mining, steel making, and machining. I learned a great deal from my male coworkers about industrial work, unionism, and how complex and contradictory consciousness can be—not only theirs but also my own. Hopefully, they learned a little from me, too.

In the 1990s, I helped to form a feminist singing group, Cross Current. This enabled me to write topical songs and participate in conferences and rallies addressing many issues. As a spin-off, I recruited a chorus of women to sing on the main stage at the 2004 March for Women's Lives in Washington, DC. It was a thrill to perform my satirical song, "If Men Could Get Pregnant—Abortion Would Be a Sacrament," based on a line originated in the sixties by Black feminist author Flo Kennedy. Not only has feminism enhanced my self-esteem and activist dedication, it also nurtured my sense of humor. Cross Current also performed for my former professor Howard Zinn when Pittsburgh's peace and justice center presented him with the Thomas Merton Award in the 1990s.

I am abundantly grateful to Female Liberation and all the wonderful sisters who have taught and inspired me and continue to give me the energy to be an activist. Sisterhood is Powerful!

Nancy: I have been a revolutionary socialist and feminist for nearly five decades.

My involvement in Female Liberation and the anti–Vietnam War movement shaped me politically, and the lessons and experiences from those years remain with me today.

I lived in the New York City area for close to thirty years, where I continued my involvement in revolutionary politics. I participated in and helped organize numerous rallies against racism and police brutality, for immigrant rights, for women's rights, and in opposition to the imperialist war moves of Washington. I joined with others in the anti-apartheid struggle in the 1970s and 1980s, demanding that companies divest their funds from apartheid South Africa.

Traveling to Cuba in 1982 and witnessing the gains of the Cuban Revolution firsthand was an inspiration. It was a lesson to me on what women can achieve with a revolutionary leadership committed to full equality for all. It also brought home to me that the liberation of women cannot be achieved under capitalism, a system based on private profit that benefits economically from keeping women as second-class citizens.

I attended the founding convention of the Coalition of Labor Union Women in 1974 in Chicago. In the years following the convention, I was a member of various industrial trade unions. I worked in the airline industry and was a member of the International Association of Machinists (IAM) for thirteen years. Working at a different airline carrier, I participated actively in support of the IAM strike at Eastern Airlines from 1989 to 1991, where militant rank-and-file unionists fought against a union-busting effort by the company.

One memorable experience I had while an airline worker was during a union contract fight. The union leadership was pushing a concessionary contract. I spoke at the union meeting of several thousand of my coworkers, mostly men, against the proposed concessions, pointing out how setting up two tiers of pay for workers divides and weakens the workforce. Several coworkers told me after the meeting that, though they didn't agree with me, they admired the fact that as a woman I spoke out.

Another experience I had was after a major airline crash in 1996. The FBI visited my workplace. This was part of an effort to turn the attention away from any concerns about how management oversaw airline safety, attempting to place the blame for the crash on the workers. Along with other coworkers, we pointed out that the FBI is not our "friend" and that we should never let them question us without a union shop steward present. Even then, we were under no obligation to provide information to the

FBI that could later be used against union members.

When the National Organization for Women issued a call for a national march for the Equal Rights Amendment in 1978, I joined 100,000 people in Washington, DC. In 1992, I marched in the 750,000-strong March for Women's Lives and again in 1995, when 200,000 demonstrated in Washington, DC, in the Rally for Women's Lives.*

In 1991 Operation Rescue announced plans to attempt to shut down clinics in Wichita, Kansas. I traveled to Wichita and, along with hundreds of others, linked arms in defense of the clinics and a woman's right to choose. We beat back Operation Rescue.

After moving to Chicago in 2009, I have worked and joined with others in defense of abortion rights. We have counter-mobilized each January in opposition to the annual so-called March for Life when right-wing opponents rally against the right to choose abortion. I participated in the January 2017 Washington, DC., Women's March, and in 2018 I marched in the Women's March in Chicago.

Along with other activists, I have joined Chicago for Abortion Rights, a local group fighting to defend *Roe v. Wade* and maintain abortion as a safe, accessible, and legal right for all.

---

*   The March for Women's Lives was held April 5, 1992. The Rally for Women's Lives occurred April 9, 1995.

FEMALE LIBERATION PHOTOGRAPHS AND LEAFLETS

The Second Wave, vol.1, no. 1, spring 1971.

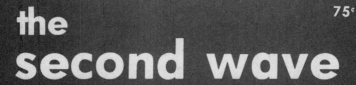

The Second Wave, vol.1, no. 2, summer 1971.

The Dialectics of Sexism

NO MORE
FUN & GAMES

ISSUE THREE

A Journal of Female Liberation

No More Fun & Games, issue 3, November 1969.

knowledge
and
control

the
issue
of
abortion

female liberation
371 somerville ave.
somerville, mass. 02143
666-8916

Pamphlet on abortion produced by Female Liberation, July 1970.

NEW ENGLAND REGIONAL FEMALE LIBERATION CONFERENCE—MAY 1969

SATURDAY, MAY 10

9:00-10:00	Registration
10:00-11:00	Karate Demonstration and Discussion of Self-Defense
11:00- 1:00	WORKSHOPS:

Sex
Being in High School
Music
Joan of Arc
Women in Socialist Countries
Family, Childcare, and
Communal Living

1:00- 2:00	Lunch (sandwiches provided)
2:00- 4:00	WORKSHOPS:

Trying to be Liberated
in an Unliberated Society
Strategy and Tactics for
a Female Liberation Movement
Women and the Movement
Women Writers

4:00-5:30	Karate Demonstration and Discussion of Self-Defense
5:30	Dinner (not provided)
8:00	Movies and Discussion (men invited) The Married Woman by Godard Miss America by Newsreel

SUNDAY, MAY 11

9:00-10:00	Coffee and Donuts
10:00-12:00	WORKSHOPS:

Black Women in a Caste Society
Women and Their Bodies
Advertising and Media as
Oppressors of Females
Workingwomen
Liberation of Welfare Mothers

12:00- 1:00	Karate Demonstration and Lunch (provided)
1:00- 3:00	WORKSHOPS:

Family as the Basic Unit of
Female Oppression
Black and White Women:
Interracial Marriages

Schedule of New England Regional Female Liberation Conference held at Emmanuel College in 1969. From the Emmanuel Focus, May 9, 1969.

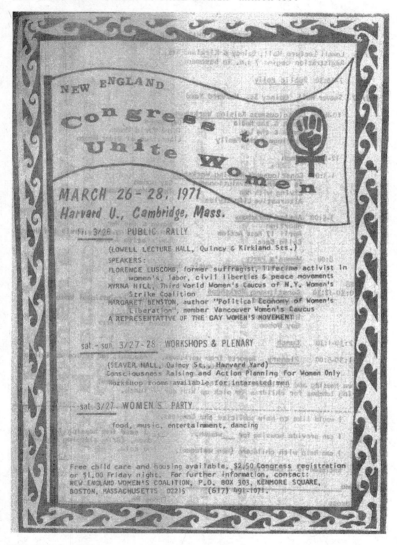

New England Congress to Unite Women leaflet, 1971

Top: Chris Hildebrand speaking at plenary session of New England Congress to Unite Women, March 1971, Harvard. Photo courtesy of Chris Hildebrand. **Bottom:** Maryanne Weathers at New England Congress to Unite Women, March 1971, Harvard. Photo courtesy of Chris Hildebrand.

FEMALE LIBERATION AT GAY PRIDE DEMONSTRATIONS—JUNE 1971

Top: Boston Gay Pride March, June 1971. In photo (from right), Claudette Begin, Ginny Hildebrand, Chris Hildebrand. Photo by Nancy Rosenstock.
Bottom: Boston Gay Pride March, June 1971. In photo (right) Claudette Begin. Photo by Nancy Rosenstock.

New York City Gay Pride March, June 1971. Photo by Nancy Rosenstock.

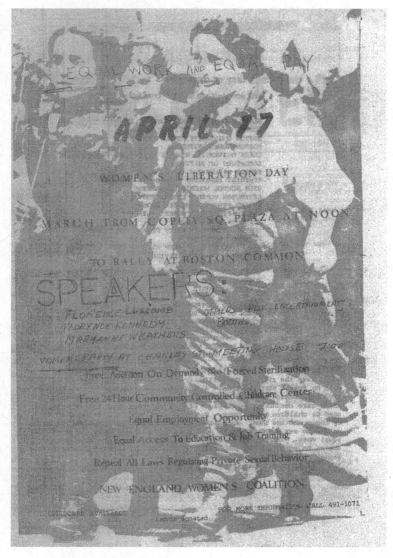

Women's Liberation Day leaflet, April 1971

Evelyn Clark at Women's Liberation Day Rally, April 1971. Photo courtesy of Evelyn Clark.

FEMALE LIBERATION AND THE ANTI-VIETNAM WAR MOVEMENT

Women's contingent leaflet for April 24, 1971, anti-Vietnam War demonstration.

Maryanne Weathers and Chris Hildebrand, selling the *Second Wave* at anti–Vietnam War demonstration, April 24, 1971, Washington, DC. Photo courtesy of Chris Hildebrand.

SELF-DEFENSE

Delpfine Welch and Pat Galligan, 1970. Photo courtesy of Delpfine Welch.

Football Won't Halve Gals, Feminist With Karate Says

By ANN CURRAN

Bearing k n a p s a c k s and wearing shirts that buttoned in the male direction and corduroy pants, the Boston Karate Team of Delpfine Welch and Pat Galligan arrived in town yesterday to participate in a two-day "Symposium on Feminism" at the University of Pittsburgh.

The girls, who wear short-cropped h a i r c u t s and no make-up, demonstrated karate last night in the Pitt Student Union and spoke on "The Need for Self-Defense."

Members of Female Liberation and the Young Socialists Alliance, neither believes, according to Pat, 22, in "women dressing to make themselves attractive to men." In a statement issued at an earlier press conference, the girls said, "Society dictates that we are female first and human beings second (if at all)."

Evidently, the duo has succeeded somewhat in reversing that order at least in the eyes of one freshman Pitt co-ed, Sheryl Morhead of Penn Hills, who thought they were boys at first.

Recommending free self-defense classes for girls in public school, Miss Galligan, a student at Emmanuel College, feels that "girls are channeled out of activities that would develop them physically."

"GIRLS WON'T break in half if they play football," the blue belt karate student continued. She looks forward to

—Post-Gazette Photo
Delpfine Welch, left, gives her old "one, two" to Pat Galligan.

Article on Female Liberation self-defense demonstration in Pittsburgh Post-Gazette, September 24, 1970. © *Pittsburgh Post-Gazette*, all rights reserved. Reprinted with permission.

help win
FREE 24 HOUR CHILD-CARE
in Cambridge

In order for women to have an equal opportunity to participate in society, to work, to study, and to be active in community life, there must be free, high quality child-care available. A large and increasing number of women have to work, just to make ends meet. There are a total of 22,000 children under 14 in Cambridge. About 4,620 of these children have mothers who work. Yet the grand total of part and full day child-care openings in Cambridge is 1,000. It is obvious that the present facilities for child care even on a day basis does not begin to fulfill the needs of Cambridge.

And children need and have a right to the best care society can provide. In a society with as many resources as ours, there is no reason for any child to be denied the opportunity to have excellent, professional supervision in clean, safe surroundings with other children to grow and identify with. Women and men who have chosen to care for young children and who are adequately trained will be much better able to deal with a childs individual needs than neighbors, older brothers and sisters, baby sitters or at worst no one at all. Too many children are left alone each day with only a house key strung around their necks.

If child-care is to be adequate for all, it must be on a 24 hour basis. Many jobs, as well as educational opportunities and emergencies, do not conveniently fit the 9 to 5 time slot. To really solve the problem, child-care must be free and available to all. Public education is free, and child-care should be seen as the same kind of social responsibility. In order to promote this sense of social responsibility and insure excellent care, facilities must be under the supervision of parents and other members of the community.

CAMBRIDGE CHILD-CARE REFERENDUM

To give the citizens of Cambridge a chance to voice their needs on the important issue of child-care, the Cambridge Child-Care Referendum Committee has begun a campaign to place a referendum for free 24 hour, parent and community controlled child-care, available to all Cambridge residents, on the ballot this November.

It is necessary to collect 3,400 valid signatures of registered voters to secure ballot status. The petitions must be submitted by the start of September, and to allow for disqualified signatures, we should collect 6-8,000. Everyone interested in winning free, 24 hour child-care in Cambridge, should help petition. Child-care will be available every Saturday at the Central School in Cambridge for parents wishing to petition.

There is much other work to be done. Please help to make this campaign a success by volunteering in whatever capacity you can.

CAMBRIDGE CHILD-CARE REFERENDUM COMMITTEE 552 Mass. Ave., Cambridge, Mass. 02139
491-0190

___ I endorse the Cambridge Child-Care Referendum
___ I would like to circulate Child-care petitions
___ I would like to so some other work on the campaign.
___ Enclosed is my contribution.

NAME _ _ _ _ _ _ _ _ _ _ _ _ _ _ _ _ _ _ _

ADDRESS _ _ _ _ _ _ _ _ _ _ _ _ _ _ _ _ _

_ _ _ _ _ _ _ _ _ _ _ _ _ _ ZIP _ _ _ _ _

PHONE _ _ _ _ _ _ _ _ _ _ _ _ _ _ _ _ _

Cambridge Child Care Referendum leaflet, 1971.

Evelyn Clark and Jeanne Lafferty, c. 1970. Photo courtesy of Evelyn Clark.

Delpfine Welch, Jeanne Lafferty and Pat Galligan, 1970. Photo courtesy of Delpfine Welch.

Evelyn Clark, c. 1970. Photo courtesy of Evelyn Clark.

Chris Hildebrand, c. 1971. Photo courtesy of Ginny Hildebrand.

Jeanne Lafferty, c. 1970. Photo courtesy of Evelyn Clark.

Boden Sandstrom (Barbara Reyes), July 1972. Photo courtesy of Boden Sandstrom.

Photo by Howard Petrick, reprinted by permission.

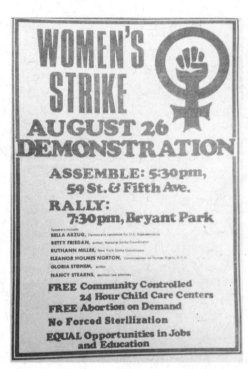

WOMEN'S STRIKE

AUGUST 26 DEMONSTRATION

ASSEMBLE: 5:30pm, 59 St. & Fifth Ave.

RALLY: 7:30pm, Bryant Park

Speakers include:

BELLA ABZUG, Democratic candidate for U.S. Representative

BETTY FRIEDAN, author, National Strike Coordinator

RUTHANN MILLER, New York Strike Coordinator

ELEANOR HOLMES NORTON, Commissioner on Human Rights, N.Y.C.

GLORIA STEINEM, author

NANCY STEARNS, abortion law attorney

FREE Community Controlled 24 Hour Child Care Centers

FREE Abortion on Demand

No Forced Sterilization

EQUAL Opportunities in Jobs and Education

Left: Leaflet for August 26, 1970 demonstration in New York City.
Bottom: August 26, 1970, New York City. Photo by Howard Petrick, reprinted by permission.

Ruthann Miller arguing with police commander prior to start of August 26, 1970 march, New York City. Photo by Howard Petrick, reprinted by permission.

Bottom: Betty Friedan and Ruthann Miller at office of August 26 coalition, New York City. Photo by Howard Petrick, reprinted by permission.

Ruthann Miller at August 26, 1970 demonstration. Photo by Howard Petrick, reprinted by permission.

Claudette Begin, Nancy Rosenstock and Boden Sandstrom, January 21, 2017, following the Women's March in Washington, DC. Photo courtesy of Nancy Rosenstock.

Maryanne Weathers, San Francisco, November 2017. Photo by Nancy Rosenstock.

FEMALE LIBERATION AT NORTHEASTERN UNIVERSITY, BOSTON, SEPTEMBER 2019

An Evening with Boston Female Liberation: Activists Look Back, 1968-1972
Tuesday, Sept. 17, 6 p.m.

A Conversation with Members of Boston Female Liberation, 1968-1972
Wednesday, Sept. 18, noon

An Evening with Boston Female Liberation: Activists Look Back, 1968-1972
Tuesday, Sept. 17, 6 p.m.
Snell Library, Room 90
Female Liberation members *Nancy Rosenstock, Delpfine Welch*, and others will present on their time in the group. Materials from Female Liberation records will be on display in the Archives and Special Collections' reading room for attendees to browse.

A Conversation with Members of Boston Female Liberation, 1968-1972
Wednesday, Sept. 18, noon
Snell Library, Room 90
Members *Nancy Rosenstock, Delpfine Welch, Evelyn Clark*, and others will take part in a panel conversation about the history of Boston Female Liberation. Lunch will be served.

Front photo courtesy of the Boston Globe Collection.
Back photo courtesy of Boston Female Liberation.

Join the Northeastern University Archives and Special Collections for two special events with members from *Boston Female Liberation*, a group of feminist activists that operated from 1968 to 1972. Female Liberation's goal was to create a community that worked for and supported women's issues in the Boston area, including self defense, equal wages, birth control, legalization of abortion, and the media's portrayal of women. Both events are free and open to the public.

Publicity for Female Liberation panel, Northeastern University, September 2019.

Top, left to right: Nancy Rosenstock, Delpfine Welch, Claudette Begin, Jeanne Lafferty at Female Liberation panel, Northeastern University, September, 2019. Photo courtesy of Kerri Vautour/Northeastern University. **Bottom:** Nancy Rosenstock at Female Liberation panel, Northeastern University, September 2019. Photo courtesy of Nancy Rosenstock.

FEMALE LIBERATION DOCUMENTS

The documents in this section all originally appeared in No More Fun and Games, the Second Wave, or the Female Liberation newsletter. The only changes made, for purposes of readability, are to correct errors of spelling and punctuation. Readers should bear in mind that these historical documents contain the language that was used at the time, which may seem jarring today. In order to maintain the integrity of these historical documents, this language has not been changed.

This statement serves as the guiding principles of Female Liberation: an independent feminist organization open to all women. It was printed in the first two issues of the Second Wave, *spring and summer 1971.*

A Statement about Female Liberation

Social attitudes toward women exist as the overt expression of centuries of female subjugation. The subordination of women is a real phenomenon, which can be pointed out in every institution and structure in society. These institutions and structures through which women are oppressed constitute a system we define as sexism, which is so deeply ingrained in every person's consciousness that most of it is not noticed or is accepted as normal. This system of sexism has also created a category of oppressed people comprising 53 percent of the human population.

Women have begun to voice their discontent with society. We have begun to talk about new alternatives. We are demanding complete control over our own lives and are beginning to act on these ideas and decisions. It is in this period of general awakening that women have come out wholly in favor of the basic rights long denied them. This insistence on the rights of women goes beyond simple legislative corrections (although we support and work for any legislation that improves our conditions here and now) and poses the question of woman's control of her life.

The nature of female oppression is such that we must question every aspect of our lives. There is nothing that we do or experience that can be separated from the fact that we are female. When we go out on the street, apply for a job, engage in any kind of social exchange or relations, society dictates that we are female first and human beings second (if at all). All women are subject to this degradation, and this is the source of our unity.

We are beginning to question every basic institution of society, including the nuclear family, because of the roles these institutions play in perpetuating our oppression.

We realize that we know nothing of female potential, since all the energy, genius, strength, and dignity of woman is refracted through the prism of sexism, which distorts and limits our possibilities in every conceivable way.

In this emerging period of feminism we have come to understand the legitimacy of our grievances. We have insisted on the right to determine the character of our movement and will not be turned back by those who feel that the oppression of females is of minor consequence. We are independent of and not a subcategory of other groups and movements.

Female Liberation is an organization which encompasses all aspects of the feminist struggle, including education, consciousness-raising activities, and action around such basic demands of the movement as child care, abortion, and equal pay. No woman is excluded from Female Liberation who is interested in the development of a strong, autonomous women's movement capable of bringing about change on every level.

It is becoming clear that this movement is reaching into every layer of the female population. We want to help mobilize the energies and power of these masses of women to fight for nothing less than our total liberation.

Why did the organization use "female" instead of "woman?" The article below takes up this question which was printed in the Second Wave, *vol. 1, no. 1, spring 1971.*

Pass the Word

by Jeanne Lafferty

Many people seem to avoid using the word "female" out of a sense of propriety, as if it were not quite polite. Some people wince when it is used. It is true that the word "female" has been used against us in the past by people whose imperfect perceptions told them that to strip away the social trappings that constitute the finished product known as "woman" would be to leave only a weak and sniveling creature, the embodiment of evil, a blot on the face of humanity (men).

Since we disagree with this analysis, our acceptance of the term comes from a different starting point. We found that the words "male" and "female" had separate origins. (This can be seen in the Latin roots *femina* and *masculus*.) We used the word "female" at first for the obvious purpose of differentiating between ourselves and the so-called opposite sex. But we also discovered that "female" easily becomes an adjective, as in "female people," "female children," "female doctor," etc., thereby implying that one's genital arrangement is not necessarily what best describes one at all times. It is more scientific to be able to distinguish between instances when one's femaleness is essential and when it is auxiliary. This is not so easily done with the word "woman," although there have been reported attempts made in this direction by people who cling to their blind distrust of so naked a concept as female.

It might be more sensible to question the word "woman," which has more social implications and innuendos. It often implies that to fulfill the requirements of one's sex is an achievement rather than a given biological fact. Somewhere in the process of striving for the rewards offered to "good women," we became aware of our humiliating role as men's willing victims, and that to be a woman meant to dress and act the part of a clown. How then could the simple biological designation of "female" be more embarrassing than the social definition of "woman"?

It should be borne in mind that it wasn't until a few years after the inception of the civil rights movement that black people discarded the term "Negro" as a suitable definition for themselves. But this rejection, when it came, was a powerful expression of the radical changes that Blacks had begun to bring about in all aspects of their lives.

It is becoming painfully clear that the word "liberation" in reference to our movement is rapidly being replaced by a small, enigmatic three-letter invention—"lib"—which makes its way into headlines, articles, leaflets, speeches, and into our everyday language. An explanation of this annoying practice is long past due. Those who have thought once about it present this usage in terms of economy and convenience. What is difficult, however, is an explanation of why these efficiency experts waited so long to save on the word "liberation." Perhaps the "National Liberation Front" is more easily converted to the "NLF," but what about the "Black Liberation movement?" And certainly "Third World Liberation" is enough of a mouthful to warrant modification. It would appear that the substitution of "lib" for "liberation" is more an attempt at diminution rather than abbreviation, a lessening rather than a shortening. Such was the case with the predominant use of "suffragette" in place of the traditional (respected) suffragist. It could be that those who favor such reductions feel that it makes the concept easier to swallow. This depends entirely on who is doing the swallowing.

The word "liberation" signifies to us freedom from oppressive social relations, sexual humiliation, fear, and daily outrages and indignities which are our lives. The word "liberation," because of its reference to all oppressed peoples, Blacks, Orientals, Third World and Working Class people, constantly relates our movement to these others. It shows lack of respect and seriousness about the Female Movement not to use this word in all its strength and dignity.

Female Liberation challenged society's norms on how women should dress and look. The article below examines the importance of this issue. It is taken from the Second Wave, *vol. 1, no. 1, spring 1971.*

The Case for Studied Ugliness

by Nancy Williamson

Recently a group of about 300 women attending a female liberation conference were described by a reporter as pre-senting an air of "studied ugliness." It was stated further that there was only one pretty girl in the group. Pretty by whose standards, I questioned. Women in the movement are fre-quently accused of being ugly (as if it were some crime that invalidates everything else we do), of defeminizing ourselves (femininity being directly proportional to the shape, size, and amount of breasts and legs showing), of having an uncouth appearance (i.e., short hair, shiny noses, unshaved legs and armpits). Frequently at public forums, orientation meetings, and in personal contacts, we are questioned about our appear-ance. Why do you wear "men's clothes?" is a frequent query. (Anything that is comfortable seems to be classified as "men's clothes.") Why don't you want to look attractive? (It seems we can't be attractive if we don't wear makeup and dresses.)

In consciously deviating from the Hollywood–Madison Avenue–Playboy norm, we have indeed affected a studied ugliness. Many of us have cut our hair and chosen to wear loose-fitting pants, shirts with high necks, sturdy shoes, rather than tight, short skirts and dresses and flimsy, fall-apart shoes for several reasons: It is more comfortable. It causes less attention on the streets. It is less abasing. It is less expensive, less time-consuming.

Any woman who has walked down the street in a mini-skirt and a lowcut blouse and high-heeled sandals knows that this attire is not only less comfortable than blue jeans and an ordinary shirt, but that it attracts far more catcalls, hooting, and leers. Leering and catcalls, though humiliating, are sometimes interpreted as flattery. If they look at me that way, I must really look beautiful today, we often think. Though this degrading behavior on the part of men is physically harmless, it is humiliating and physically damaging to women to be subjected to it day after day, wherever we go. We become public property with no privacy and no recourse but to hang our heads and mince by. Furthermore, it becomes more and more difficult to dismiss verbal harassment as harmless as the crimes against women in this country spiral higher and higher. For every group of men who stand around on street corners and leer at women, there is at least one rapist lurking nearby. For every successful rape there are many thwarted ones. We can no longer afford to provoke men by the way we dress. This constant threat of physical violence is a primary reason for our being *careful* in choosing the clothes we wear when going out alone.

And as for going out alone, which we are often advised not to do, it is humiliating to feel that we are not capable of taking care of ourselves, that we have to have some man there by our side to defend us from the lurking masses. Clothes present an image; we can perhaps ward off men by not provoking them with sexy clothes. But no matter what we wear, any woman is subject to harassment and attack on any street in any city or rural area in this country in the daytime or at night. Clothes are not the answer to the threat of physical violence. A society that does not tolerate sexual oppression and frees all people from the threat of violence is the only solution. Yet clothes are one means of preserving dignity at this time in history.

Our style of dress is less expensive, less time-consuming than the more traditional feminine attire. Curlers, cosmetics, girdles, high heels, and other stifling female gear has hampered our physical freedom and kept us from developing healthy bodies, as well as consumed hours of our time. The closet full of dresses that is necessary when one has to have a different dress every day and for every occasion requires money and time to acquire and maintain. The time spent in shaving legs and arms three or four times a week, curling, washing, and pampering long hair alone amounts to the time it takes to read a book, go to a movie, or just sit and think. Which is more important? And why should hair on a man be virile, while hair on a woman (other than long silky tresses on her head) is repulsive? All the other time-consuming beautifiers—plucking eyebrows, making up faces, sitting in beauty salons—that have come to define our identities and consume our lives are not just irrelevant to us, they are detrimental to our mental health. We are being used by the image-makers and profit-takers of this country to promote their own interests. Cosmetics alone are a multimillion-dollar industry. Why do we think we need these things? Because we've been told for so long in so many subtle ways that we do. It was not in obeisance to beauty alone that Helena Rubenstein* founded her famous salon, or that all the contemporary male fashion makers have successfully fostered the image of the powdered, perfumed female animal. Our pockets as well as our minds have been picked.

There are strong pressures in the society for women to conform to the accepted standards of fashion. Women who

---

*   Helena Rubenstein, founder of a cosmetics company in the early 1900s.

work must continue to dress traditionally. Secretaries cannot go to work in blue jeans or slacks without arousing hostility and often dismissal. Waitresses, restaurant hostesses, airline stewardesses have to wear uniforms which are sometimes degrading. Many women in these positions resent being told what they have to wear; they do not like having to spend a large portion of their already too meagre salaries (what employer ever gives a secretary a clothes allowance?) for uncomfortable, sexist dresses, stockings that run the first time they are worn, shoes that cause callouses and backaches. As more and more women begin to chafe at the degradation of having to dress up like china dolls on display for the male population, there will be pressure on employers to allow us to dress as we choose. Determining one's mode of dress is a constitutional right upheld by a Supreme Court decision. Employers can no longer legally require women to wear certain kinds of clothes (or men to have certain hairstyles). In rejecting the popularized image of the beautiful female, we should constantly demand the right of all women to create their own physical images.

In dressing contrary to social standards, we are rejecting the image of the bejeweled, bedecked woman; we are not only refusing to fritter away our time, energy, and money noncreatively, supporting a coterie of male fashion pimps who have created a false and humiliating image of femaleness, we are actively discrediting that image; we are asserting our human dignity and our right to control our lives. Ugliness, whether studied or real, is in the eye of the beholder, and for us the values of the male beholder in this society are totally irrelevant at this time.

Is women's liberation only for white women? Such a view was commonly presented in the media and was echoed at the time by some men in the Black liberation movement. This groundbreaking article looks at this question. It was published in No More Fun and Games, *issue 2, February 1969.*

An Argument for Black Women's Liberation as a Revolutionary Force

by Maryanne Weathers

"Nobody can fight your battles for you; you have to do it yourself." This will be the premise used for the time being for stating the case for Black women's liberation, although certainly it is the least significant. Black women, at least the Black women I have come in contact with in the movement, have been expounding all their energies in "liberating" Black men. (If you yourself are not free, how can you "liberate" someone else?) Consequently, the movement has practically come to a standstill. Not entirely due, however, to wasted energies, but adhering to basic false concepts rather than revolutionary principles, and at this stage of the game we should understand that if it is not revolutionary it is false.

We have found that Women's Liberation is an extremely emotional issue, as well as an explosive one. Black men are still parroting the master's prattle about male superiority. This now brings us to the very pertinent question: how can we seriously discuss reclaiming our African heritage—cultural living modes which clearly refute not only patriarchy and matriarchy, but our entire family structure as we know it? African tribes live communally where households, let alone heads of households, are non-existent.

It is really disgusting to hear Black women talk about giving Black men their manhood—or allowing them to get it. This is degrading to other Black women and thoroughly insulting to Black men (or at least it should be). How can someone "give" one something as personal as one's adulthood? That's precisely like asking the beast for your freedom. We also chew the fat about standing behind our men. This forces me to the question: are we women or leaning posts and props? It sounds as if we are saying if we come out from behind him, he'll fall down. To me, these are clearly maternal statements and should be closely examined.

Women's Liberation should be considered as a strategy for an eventual tie-up with the entire revolutionary movement consisting of women, men, and children. We are now speaking of real revolution (armed). If you cannot accept this fact purely and without problems, examine your reactions closely. We are playing to win and so are they. Vietnam is simply a matter of time and geography.

Another matter to be discussed is the liberation of children from a sick, slave culture. Although we don't like to see it, we are still operating within the confines of the slave culture. Black women use their children for their own selfish needs of worth and love. We try to live our lives, which are too oppressing to bear, through our children and thereby destroy them in the process. Obviously the much-acclaimed plaudits of the love of the Black mother has some discrepancies. If we allow ourselves to run from the truth, we run the risk of spending another 400 years in self-destruction. Assuming, of course, the beast would tolerate us that long, and we know he wouldn't.

Women have fought with men, and we have died with

men in every revolution, more timely [recently] in Cuba, Algeria, China, and now in Vietnam. If you notice, it is a woman heading the "Peace Talks" in Paris for the NLF. What is wrong with Black women? We are clearly the most oppressed and degraded minority in the world, let alone the country. Why can't we rightfully claim our place in the world?

Realizing fully what is being said, you should be warned that the opposition to liberation will come from everyplace, particularly from other women and from Black men. Don't allow yourselves to be intimidated any longer with this nonsense about the "matriarchy" of Black women.* Black women are not matriarchs, but we have been forced to live in abandonment and been used and abused. The myth of the matriarchy must stop, and we must not allow ourselves to be sledgehammered by it any longer—not if we are serious about change and ridding ourselves of the wickedness of this alien culture. Let it be clearly understood that Black women's liberation is not anti-male; any such sentiment or interpretation as such cannot be tolerated. It must be taken clearly for what it is—pro-human, for all peoples.

The potential for such a movement is boundless. Whereas in the past only a certain type of Black people have been attracted to the movement—younger people, radicals, and militants. The very poor, the middle class, older people, and women have not become aware or have not been able

---

*   The 1965 Moynihan Report on "The Negro Family: The Case for National Action," written by then assistant secretary of labor Daniel Patrick Moynihan, examined the causes of poverty in urban Black communities. He placed a large share of the blame on the rise of families led by single mothers. A section of the report, titled "Matriarchy," stated: "A fundamental fact of Negro American family life is the often reversed roles of husband and wife."

to translate their awareness into action. Women's liberation offers such a channel for these energies.

Even though middle-class Black women may not have suffered the brutal suppression of poor Black people, they most certainly have felt the scourge of the male superiority-oriented society as women, and would be more prone to help in alleviating some of the conditions of our more oppressed sisters by teaching, raising awareness and consciousness, verbalizing the ills of women and this society, helping to establish communes.

Older women have a wealth of information and experience to offer and would be instrumental in closing the communications gap between the generations. To be Black and to tolerate this jive about discounting people over 30 is madness.

Poor women have knowledge to teach us all. Who else in this society sees more and is more realistic about ourselves and this society and about the faults that lie within our own people than our poor women? Who else could profit and benefit from a communal setting that could be established than these sisters? We must let the sisters know that we are capable, and some of us already do love them. We women must begin to unabashedly learn to use the word "love" for one another. We must stop the petty jealousies, the violence that we Black women have for so long perpetrated on one another about fighting over this man or the other. (Black men should have better sense [than] to encourage this kind of destructive behavior.) We must turn to ourselves and one another for strength and solace. Just think for a moment what it would be like if we got together and internalized our own 24-hour-a-day communal centers, knowing our children would be safe and loved constantly. Not to mention what it would do for everyone's egos, especially the children. Women should not have to be enslaved by this society's concept of motherhood through their children, and then the kids suffer through a mother's resentment of it by beatings, punishment, and rigid discipline. All one has to do is look at the statistics of Black women who are rapidly filling the beast's mental institutions to know that the time for innovation and change and creative thinking is here. We cannot sit on our behinds waiting for someone else to do it for us. We must save ourselves.

We do not have to look at ourselves as someone's personal sex objects, maids, babysitters, domestics, and the like in exchange for a man's attention. Men hold this power, along with that of the breadwinner, over our heads for these services and that's all it is—servitude. In return we torture him and fill him with insecurities about his manhood and literally force him to "cat" and "mess around," bringing in all sorts of conflicts. This is not the way really human people live. This is whitey's thing. And we play the game with as much proficiency as he does.

If we are going to bring about a better world, where best to begin than with ourselves? We must rid ourselves of our own hang-ups, before we can begin to talk about the rest of the world, and we mean the world and nothing short of just that. (Let's not kid ourselves.) We will be in a position soon of having to hook up with the rest of the oppressed peoples of the world who are involved in liberation just as we are, and we had better be ready to act.

All women suffer oppression, even white women, particularly poor white women, and especially Indian, Mexican, Puerto Rican, Oriental, and Black American women, whose oppression is tripled by any of the above mentioned. But we do have female oppression in common. This means that we can begin to talk to other women with this common factor and start building links with them and thereby build and transform the revolutionary force we are now beginning to amass. This is what Dr. King was doing. We can no longer allow ourselves to be duped by the guise of racism. Any time the white man admits to something, you know he is trying to cover something else up. We are all being exploited, even the white middle class, by the few people in control of this entire world. And to keep the real issue clouded, he keeps us at one another's throats with this racism jive. Although whites are most certainly racist, we must understand that they have been programmed to think in these patterns to divert their attention. If they are busy fighting us, then they have no time to question the policies of the war being run by this government. With the way the elections went down, it is clear that they are as powerless as the rest of us. Make no question about it, folks, this fool knows what he is doing. This man is playing the death game for money and power, not because he doesn't like us. He could care less one way or the other. But think for a moment if we all go together and just walked on out. Who would fight his wars, who would run his police state, who would work his factories, who would buy his products?

We women must start this thing rolling.

A common view among many supporters of Black liberation when this article was written was that Black women should be opposed to abortion because it was genocide. This argument is clearly rejected in this important article by Weathers. It appeared in the Second Wave, *vol. 1, no. 2, summer 1971.*

Black Women and Abortion

by Maryanne Weathers

The subject of abortion has finally come to the *practical* attention of the black community. By practical, we mean viewing abortion or terminated pregnancy as a functional alternative to an otherwise disastrous situation.

For so long, contraception has been accessible to only those who could afford it: white women with the financial means and contacts. For black women, nothing could be further removed. Pregnancy for us, in too many cases, has meant a one-way ticket to the nowhere place of the welfare rolls. The racist-class oppression has been our major obstacle, but by no means the only one. There are also the psychological manifestations of being the most exploited and oppressed sex-race-class in America. We have always been on the bottom and locked outside, forced into the desperate state of isolation, consequently feeling that if it wasn't for this little love inside me, I damn sure wouldn't have no love at all. ENTER JESUS.

We have always maintained, and do so now, that the only true Christians in America are black people. Nowhere does one find a more sincere adherence to the credo, historically, than among us. This is especially true of black women.

Aside from the fantasy of the family as a source of all one's just rewards, the concept of the Lord and all that goes with it has been the only possible source of hope, redemption, and salvation. This then adds still another cause for pain in the dilemma of an unwanted pregnancy. What will my Jesus say? What will my family say? Will this make them angry? Will this force me even deeper and further away? The obvious answer, after four hundred years of heavenly, paternal, and maternal pronouncements, day in and day out, is HELL YES! But we are finally beginning to see that if He hasn't done anything about anything else, He probably isn't going to make any sudden moves at this late date about a step towards practical reality and survival. As far as the family is concerned, they are neither eager nor able to take on the added expense of an extra mouth to feed and body to clothe.

Black men have done little else than lend insult to injury. For a man, any man, to encourage, even force, a woman to breed against her valid wishes is nothing short of barbaric. We do not subscribe to the idea that abortion in the black community is genocide. If that program is controlled by the community, it is not genocide. The laws as they stand now are genocidal, forcing women to die at the hands of butchers.

Black women must and will decide everything concerning our lives. No man, no state, no society will ever again dare to intrude or dictate how we live. We have our own clear-thinking consciousness, everyday instincts of survival, which have proven to be invincible. This, coupled with generations of historical experiences to call upon when necessary, outweighs anything anyone else may superimpose on us. All we need now is organization, exchange of information between all sisters, and some aggressive (don't be afraid of the word) assertion and determination to acquire our rights and permanent liberation.

*In 1971, abortion was illegal. This article deals with the centrality
of this issue, and why having control over our bodies is fundamental
to our liberation. It was published in the* Second Wave, *vol. 1, no. 3,
1971.*

Abortion: A Feminist Perspective

by Nancy Williamson

From a feminist perspective, the repeal of abortion laws
means far more than the right to legal abortions. If the abortion issue ended with the simple matter of a woman's right to
terminate a pregnancy, the laws would probably have been
repealed long ago or they would never have existed.

The question of abortion and a woman's right to obtain
one directly threatens the institutions of the family, the
church, and the state; in short, the whole sexist society in
which we live. We are not asking for abortion. We are asking
for control of our bodies and thus our lives. Once abortion
laws are repealed, our bodies will no longer be controlled
from without. They will be controlled from within—through
our own choice, through the dictates of our minds. Woman
will control herself. She will not be controlled by the state.

Repealing all abortion laws is not a moral issue where
the state is concerned. It is a political issue. It is a question
of survival. Who survives? Us or them? That is the question.
In matters of morality, the state intervenes only in its own
interest, not in the interest of the individual. From Vietnam, Kent State, Jackson State, to the current Attica Prison
incident, we see that when it is a question of morality—of the

rights of the individual, of the sacredness of human life—the political apparatus in this country is blind to any other interest than preserving its own power.

Seven thousand or more women die each year from botched illegal abortions. 350,000 more end up with serious complications. The incidence of reported child abuse in New York City went up 549 percent in the past five years. That's a hard figure to assimilate, but if you've talked to a nurse or a doctor or a social worker, or [have] been one yourself and seen children who've been beaten with instruments ranging from bare fists to baseball bats, children burned over open flames, gas burners, and cigarette lighters, strangled or suffocated with pillows or plastic bags, drowned, then it's easier to understand what the statistics mean. These are unwanted children. These are children usually born into poverty—60 percent of battered children are from poverty homes.

Who in the state legislatures is worrying about the morality of child abuse? Who of the fetus protectors is worried about the already living children, living in fear and dread, hunger and neglect? As long as there are abortion laws and inadequate, unsafe, unavailable contraception, the moral injustice is being perpetrated by the state against women and children.

It's us that are not surviving now. And we have an abortion movement in this country aimed at changing the situation.

From the beginning of the feminist movement, abortion has been a key issue—distinct but inseparable from the other basic demands of the women's movement, i.e., child care, equal pay for equal work, freedom of sexual expression, and so on. They are all equally important. They are all interrelated. They all involve a woman's right to control her life.

Why has abortion rather than any of the other basic issues become prominent this year? The question of abortion law repeal has become a prominent one not because feminists chose to make it so, not because a small group of us sat down one day and said, let's make abortion the issue this year.

We didn't choose abortion. It chose us. There was an abortion reform movement before there was a women's liberation movement. It was made up of doctors, lawyers, sociologists, social workers, clergymen, professors and writers, but most of all women who saw that abortion law repeal is a life-or-death issue, and that something has to be done about it now.

Hundreds of people have been working for years to have those laws changed, and there have been some victories along the way in several states. Nevertheless, in most states there are laws on the books that prevent women from obtaining safe, legal abortions easily. And in states where it is possible to get legal abortions, they are generally available only to middle- and upper-class women. 80 percent of legal abortions are performed on white middle- and upper-class women, while 80 percent of women who die in New York City from illegal abortions are Black or Puerto Rican, and the overall number of deaths from illegal abortions is among poor white, black, and Third World women. The financial status of a woman determines the availability of an abortion. Thus, feminists see not only the need for repeal of all abortion laws, but for free abortion on demand.

Because there is another large group of people outside the women's movement organizing around the issue of abortion at this time, it is important for feminists to join forces with them, to make a large movement which will win the repeal of these laws immediately. We can influence the abortion movement in a feminist direction, we can see that the laws are repealed sooner, and we can see that those people who are already involved in the abortion movement will be exposed to feminist ideas on other questions involving women's rights.

There is a fear in the women's movement that the abortion issue will become monumentally important to the exclusion of all other feminist demands. The analogy is made between the suffragist movement and the abortion campaign.

The early feminist movement died after women got the vote. So, say some pessimistic feminists, will our movement die with the repeal of abortion laws. The fear is unfounded. There is a fundamental difference between the current women's movement and the suffragist movement, one that needs to be reiterated and remembered when thinking about the abortion struggle—and that is that this current movement is and has been from its inception a multi-issue movement which began at a much more sophisticated level than the early single-issue suffragist movement. We began with demands for child care, abortion, equal pay, freedom of sexual expression—all demands that imply a restructuring of society, demands that threaten the most cherished institution in the society on which the oppression of women is founded—the family.

The early feminist movement began as a single-issue movement—to get the vote—and it ended when the vote was won, for various reasons, but primarily because women thought that when they won the vote they would be able to achieve other feminist demands through the political system. That did not happen. Is there anyone who thinks that with the repeal of abortion laws, any of the other demands of the women's movement will be satisfied? I doubt it. That does not make the struggle to repeal abortion laws any less important. We know that abortion law repeal is only the first step in the total process of freeing women from sexist oppression. We know that women's liberation means a total restructuring of patriarchal society. We know that the winning of one of our demands—the repeal of all abortion laws—is just the beginning. But it is an important beginning, for once we control our reproductive organs, we are on the way to controlling our lives.

7,000 women dead each year from illegal abortions. 350,000 maimed. 1,500,000 illegal abortions yearly, most of them involving shame, degradation, humiliation, fear, and a lot of money.

But statistics don't mean much personally, so I want to talk in personal terms for a few minutes. One out of four of us has had or will have an abortion. Your roommate. Your best friend. You. Real people that you see every day, not just some statistics compiled by a Gallup poll on women you never saw or knew, but your friends and people you love.

I am one of the [one in] four who has had an abortion. I was lucky to have had a good experience. It was illegal, but it was relatively inexpensive, and it was a good job. I had no complications—either physical or mental. I think of it as one of the luckiest breaks I ever had.

I was also, however, one of the millions of teenagers in the U.S. who bears a so-called illegitimate child. That was a different experience altogether. Of all the experiences I've had in my life, that was the most psychically damaging. At fifteen years old I was pregnant and without recourse to anything but a so-called home for unwed mothers. I lived completely isolated from society for nine months. My parents sent me there very early in the pregnancy because they wanted to be sure no one knew about it. I took care of the child for a month after it was born and then it was given up for adoption. My high school education was interrupted. I was not allowed to know what happened to the child. I internalized for years the guilt that society imposes on such offenders. (At that time I had no idea how many other people were experiencing the same kind of thing; I thought it only happened to me and a few others.) Every year hundreds of young women find themselves in this situation. A legal abortion at that time and competent sympathetic medical and psychiatric counselling could save years of suffering. A society that provided adequate birth control information and contraception to young people, a society wherein there was no stigma against children born outside marriage could eliminate the kind of suffering that I went through at fifteen. Teenage boys today don't know or care any more about contraception than they did when I was fifteen, yet I am sure they are even more sophisticated at seducing young women than my contemporaries were, for the figures on so-called illegitimate pregnancies increase yearly and these pregnancies are suffered primarily by young women.

Women cannot afford to go on accepting the mental and physical suffering imposed by unwanted pregnancies. We cannot continue to let unwanted, unloved children be born. We need free abortion on demand for all women, and we also need competent, feminist medical and psychiatric counselling and safe, 100-percent-effective contraception. None of these alone is enough. All these together will help women make the first step toward controlling our lives.

What the women's movement needs now is a major victory. Feminists haven't won a major victory since we won the vote. In many areas we've been regressing. The wage gap between men and women has increased for 25 years. There are fewer female PhDs now than in 1940. Forty percent of the workforce is women and yet women's average income is below poverty level. In 1940, 45 percent of professional and technical workers were women; in 1968 only 37 percent.

It's time we understood that voting is not where the action is. At this time in history—this year with the beginning of the national abortion campaign—it's possible to win an overwhelming victory and to show the government once and for all that women mean business. Actually, I think they know that we mean business. And I think they know how important the issue of abortion is in the overall scheme of things. They know it's not just abortion we want, but a total restructuring of society, a society that is life-protecting rather than life-destroying.

We can go on dying from illegal abortions, bearing unwanted children, and suffering the guilt and pain and social stigma that is imposed upon us by this government. Or we can make a concentrated effort right now to change the laws in every state in the country. We didn't choose the abortion issue. It chose us. But the final choice is ours. We have to choose to work to repeal the laws right now and we have to choose in massive numbers. A handful of well-meaning doctors and lawyers and feminists can't do it. It's going to take a mass movement of women with a feminist perspective to repeal those laws and guarantee abortion to every woman who needs one.

One of the hallmarks of Female Liberation was understanding that, as this article puts it, "The attacks on women will stop only when it becomes as dangerous to attack a woman as it is to attack another man." This article appeared in No More Fun and Games, *issue 3, November 1969.*

Females and Self-Defense

by Pat Galligan and Delpfine Welch

The ever-increasing rate of the traditional crimes against women has prompted women's magazines and newspapers to issue warnings and offer advice to their female readers. We are warned not to go out unaccompanied after dark, but if we must venture out alone, we are advised to carry alarms, mace, nailfiles, to avoid enticing clothing, and of course if attacked—scream so some passing man will come to our rescue.

The crimes against women are the most blatant expression of the pervasive attitude of men towards women. While some of us have not experienced the extreme, all of us have been subjected to the more "harmless" forms—being handled, whistled at, pinched, hooted at. You don't treat an equal human being like that. Any female not under the "protection" of a male is "free game." If she's not private property, then she's public property.

We have depended on males to "protect" us too long. The right to protect is also the right to oppress. It is time that all females learn to defend themselves.

Males are taught how to take care of themselves while growing up. Females are systematically denied this right. Our culture does not allow women to develop strength. Girls are not supposed to do physical things. The result is that women are pitifully weak. The psychological consequences are of even greater significance. Women feel they should be weak, that they need a man to protect them.

Women's physical weakness and its psychological consequences can only be overcome through developing their bodies. Of the various forms of self-defense, karate enables you to become consciously aware of your physical potential by teaching you to mobilize your whole body. Only when we have gained the self-confidence that comes through developing our physical potential and exercising it will we be able to gain any individual mobility.

It is a basic and immediate necessity that all women be given access to free self-defense instruction. Individual women should not have to pay to learn how to defend themselves. It is not an individual problem. Women should demand that free self-defense instruction be provided by towns, schools, businesses, welfare departments . . . all institutions which have direct control over women's lives.

The attacks on women will stop only when it becomes as dangerous to attack a woman as it is to attack another man.

Female Liberation members spoke at many anti–Vietnam war protests and conferences, linking the fight for women's liberation to opposition to the war. The speech below was published in the Female Liberation newsletter, July 12, 1971.

Feminism and the Anti–War Movement

by Pat Galligan

(Speech given at the opening session of the National Peace Action Conference, July 2–4, 1971, New York City)

I want to talk about the relation of the Feminist Movement to the Anti-War Movement.

A recent opinion poll showed that over 70% of the women in this country are opposed to the war in Southeast Asia. It's easy to understand why so many women are against the war. Many of us have lost husbands, fathers, brothers, sons, lovers, or close friends. War-induced inflation is taking its toll on our standard of living. We know of the incredible destruction and suffering American armies have caused. We know of the brutal massacres. And for what? To protect these people from the evils of Communism? At least that's what we've been told. Of course, women are against this war.

We in the Feminist Movement—young and old, workers and students, married and single, straight and gay, third world and white—are no different from the rest of our sisters. We are all interested in the quality of life, not in the destruction of lives.

Many of us in the Feminist Movement have come to

understand that it is not enough to be opposed to the war. We are beginning to see that the struggle against the war is a crucial part of our struggle for liberation. We have to participate in and build the Anti-War Movement.

Female Liberation publicized and participated in the demonstrations of October 31 and May 5. We helped to organize the United Women's Contingent for April 24. We urged the 800 sisters who receive our newsletter to attend these demonstrations. We have had speakers at rallies and conferences. We are publishing an anti-war speech by our sister Nancy Williamson in our magazine, THE SECOND WAVE. We are trying to involve women coming into our movement in the fight against the war. We also bring feminist ideas to women already in the Anti-War Movement. Why are we doing this?

We see that the same government which denies the people of Southeast Asia the right to self-determination also denies women the right to control our own bodies and lives. In April, President Nixon announced his opposition. He declared that his reverence for "the sanctity of life" extended even to the unborn in womb—that is of course, as long as it isn't the womb of a Vietnamese woman.

How can that man talk about the sanctity of life when he has ordered and continues to order the murder and mutilation of countless Southeast Asians? He upholds the rights of the fetus while 7,000 women die each year in this country from botched, illegal abortions. The hypocrisy we encounter at the centers of power is appalling.

The American military system deliberately tries to turn G.I.s into mindless murderers. This system, which leads to the Calley massacres of women and children and the day-to-day ravaging of Vietnamese women, is an extension of sexist ideology which dehumanizes all females. Women are raped and butchered here as well as in Vietnam.

Compare the treatment of Lt. Calley, a confessed and convicted murderer, with that of Angela Davis, who allegedly bought a gun that allegedly was used to murder.* Compare the treatment of Lt. Calley with that of the women who have rotted in New York's House of Detention.

Female Liberation is waging a petition campaign to win free, 24-hour, community-controlled child care centers in Cambridge. Officials are bewildered—where will the money come from? The government spends billions each year on the war and yet there is no money for child care—or education, or housing, or medical care.

The government dumps "surplus" food in the ocean while people starve. It pays farmers not to farm and gives oil barons money because someday their wells will run dry. And yet, there is no money for child care.

One of the sexist myths about women is that we are irrational. No, we are very rational. It is the government that is irrational as it carries out its policies of waste and destruction. American women and the people of Southeast Asia

---

* Lieutenant William Calley Jr. was charged with involvement in the March 1968 My Lai massacre, an act of mass murder in which US troops killed some five hundred Vietnamese men, women, and children—many of the women being gang-raped before they were murdered. Calley was convicted of killing twenty-two villagers and was originally given a life sentence but served only three and a half years under house arrest.

Black liberation activist Angela Davis was accused of having supplied weapons for an August 1970 raid on a California courtroom. Given an atmosphere of hysteria prevailing at the time in which she likely would have been railroaded to prison, Davis chose to avoid arrest by going underground. Put on the FBI's "Most Wanted" list, she was arrested in October 1970 and held in solitary confinement as a dangerous criminal. At her trial in 1972, Davis was found not guilty.

have the same enemy—the U.S. government. Our struggle is the same. We are all fighting to control our lives.

Women want to end this war. Will the government end it for us? The Pentagon Papers have shown that we cannot trust this government to end the war. If we want the war to end, we will have to end it. Writing to Nixon or the Congress will not end the war. Electing "peace candidates" will not end the war. We have to mobilize more and more people in the streets in massive demonstrations to demand an immediate end to the war.

We in the Feminist Movement have learned much from the Anti-War Movement. Many of us first became radicalized over the issue of the war. Huge anti-war demonstrations were examples for August 26 actions across the country. August 26 was the turning point of our movement. Thousands of women marched for feminist demands. The United Women's Contingent for April 24 was a preview of the kind of national feminist demonstration we will have.

We are building a national coalition to repeal all abortion laws. We are trying to reach out to build the broadest possible support. We hope to build massive demonstrations to demand the repeal of abortion laws. The Anti-War Movement provides us with the example to do this.

Feminists support the Anti-War Movement in a very principled way. We are not guilt-baited into the anti-imperialist struggle because it is more worthy or more revolutionary than the feminist struggle. We recognize the validity of our own movement. We understand the revolutionary nature of feminism. Our movement will not be subordinated to any other movement. We support the Anti-War Movement because ending the war is a necessary step toward our liberation.

Women have been the silent majority throughout history. Those days are over. More and more women are becoming vocal. They are standing up and fighting to control their lives. They will no longer silently, passively accept oppression and they now see how the war is connected with their oppression.

We in Female Liberation call on all our sisters throughout the country to get out of the kitchens and into the streets, to show the government what we, the no-longer-silent majority, want.

We want the priorities of this country to be reversed so that the tremendous wealth we possess will be used to serve the needs of the people and not to line the pockets of a few.

We want a society and a world that are conducive to building decent human relationships.

The first step toward getting what we want is ending the war. We want child care, not warfare.

We demand immediate, total, and unconditional withdrawal of all troops from Southeast Asia.

We want an end to this damned war, and we want it NOW.

Different political perspectives arose in Female Liberation in the fall of 1970: Should the organization work toward building a mass women's movement open to all or should the path of small group cell orientation continue? The open letter below takes up developments that arose from these differing views. It was printed in the Female Liberation newsletter, December 1970.

Which Way for Female Liberation

September 1970

Dear Sisters,

As most of you know, Female Liberation has been growing tremendously during the past few months, especially since we opened our new office at 1126 Boylston St. in Boston. Beginning with our wholehearted participation in the August 26th Coalition, we began to encourage all women to come to Female Liberation meetings and function actively as part of the Women's movement.

This kind of development was a big change for Female Liberation, since we had always been a small group and never encouraged other women to become involved in our group. Although many of the women who were early activists in Female Liberation are still active members today, we find that a tiny grouping of sisters from the older, closed group are now opposing the fact that Female Liberation has become a much larger, active organization. They decided that they want to separate from all the activities of the office and the Monday night business meetings, where we make all our major decisions democratically.

We believe that this is their right and feel that the movement is broad enough to include every kind of group. We absolutely defend the right of any group to be whatever the members determine.

The problem occurred because those few demanded complete control over the Journal and the finances of Female Liberation and refused to abide by the decisions of the business meeting. They put forward their claim on the basis of large financial contributions made to the Female Liberation checking account in the past by one of them. Many women in the movement give *whatever they* can in terms of both time and money, yet we feel that no one has more right than another to make the political decisions that affect our lives. They also asked that we change our name from Female Liberation to something else. They stated that they did not recognize the authority of the weekly business meeting where the decisions of the active Female Liberation group are made.

At the Monday night business meeting on November 16th attended by 35 women, we thoroughly discussed these proposals. It was the feeling of the group present that Female Liberation is a group that belongs to all its members and supporters, not to single individuals, and that the work that lies before us can only move forward if we treat each other as sisters and make our decisions democratically. We voted unanimously against giving them the money, changing the name of the group, and accepting a closed editorial board. Everyone agreed that these 4 sisters would be welcome to participate in the Journal and be represented on the editorial board. Immediately after the meeting we called them to inform them of our decisions and we urged them to come to the next business meeting to see if we couldn't work out something more satisfactory together. This proposal was rejected, the reason being that they didn't recognize the business meeting.

To our amazement, three of these people organized a raid on the Female Liberation office sometime between the hours of 2 and 9 a.m., Tuesday, Nov. 17th. The following items were taken: the mimeograph machine, the typewriter, two staplers, the movie projector, all the business files, all copies of the mailing lists for the newsletter, journal orders, etc. ALL THE TAPES FROM THE CONFERENCE LAST WEEKEND, $500.00 worth of Journals, all boxes of the Baltimore Journals, and Notes from the Second Year. Later in the day we found out that they went to the Post Office to divert all Female Liberation mail to one of their homes. After this we discovered that these people organized an illegal entry into the home of Female Liberation member Barbara Reyes and stole $5,000 worth of literature that was in storage in her foyer. They based their "right" to do this on the fact that one of their names appears on the lease to the office. When members of Female Liberation found this office in August, the landlord required the signature of an individual, although it was clearly understood that the office was for Female Liberation and its activities. Female Liberation has paid the rent every month from the very beginning. We have repeatedly requested that these sisters meet with the business meeting or representatives of the business meeting to see if a compromise can be worked out.

However, let it be known that we will take whatever steps are necessary to protect and defend Female Liberation, our organization. We would like very much to see this kind of behavior ended, because it only hurts the movement and disrupts everybody's work. We encourage *everyone* to attend business meetings. We are dedicated to continuing the activities of Female Liberation.

We have recently taken steps to become a legally recognized non-profit organization, as many other groups do.

This was done in order to protect Female Liberation, both the name and our mail, as well as to facilitate purchasing and renting equipment and space. This was not designed to limit membership. Neither was it intended to prevent other people or groups from using the name Female Liberation, but only to make sure we can use the name and to safeguard our rights in the future.

Right now there are about 40 women who attend meetings each week as well as about 700 who participate in our activities and receive the weekly Newsletter. The level of support for these activities is very high, as witnessed by the fact that hundreds of women responded to our request for money to continue the newsletter two months ago. ($500.00 has been collected from that appeal.)

New campus chapters have sprung up this year at B.U. and Northeastern. Female Liberation has sent speakers to almost every university in the area, numerous high schools, and is now, at the request of women at U. Mass., Amherst, and Clark, helping to get groups started at these schools. We have spoken before a great number of groups ranging from high school women to the YWCAs and a young marrieds church club. We have reached thousands of people through our participation on radio and T.V. shows as well as through our literature, which we constantly put out to help fill the needs of a growing movement. We have distributed over 125,000 leaflets since August 26th, compiled a pamphlet on abortion, issued a selection of reprints from our last two Journals. We are planning a pamphlet on the Equal Rights Amendment. We printed up two articles on the issue of abortion as concerns Black and Brown Women, we distributed much of the literature put out by other groups. We had planned to put out a fifth edition of *A Journal of Female Liberation* and have started work on a new Feminist magazine that could be published on a regular basis and deal with the ideas and issues of the day.

Female Liberation has weekly orientation meetings, Thursday nights at 8:00 at the office. Study and consciousness-raising groups have also been meeting there. A child-care group has developed, and several suburban groups have been meeting in their towns and using the office as a coordinating center. Female Liberation sponsored a Teach-In on abortion at B.U., and a panel at the office on the Equal Rights Amendment. We were asked to send speakers and a karate team to conferences in Pittsburgh and Washington D.C., where we met many new sisters who have remained in touch with us and attended our own conference two weeks ago. We have built up a bookstore and are in the process of establishing a Feminist library. We have new buttons and are carrying posters and stickers. Last week we sponsored a Female Liberation conference, which was held at B.U., to provide an opportunity for women to talk about their ideas and discuss how we can get together and build a movement. Almost 500 women, many of them very new to the movement, participated in the conference. The atmosphere was of serious political discussion as well as a powerful feeling of sisterhood. Out of some of the conference workshops came: a campus coordinating committee to take care of inter-school activities and help initiate new groups; a high school committee was formed along the same lines. Out of the Black and Third World Women's workshop came the formation of the Black and Third World Women's Alliance, involving about 15 women committed to participating in the group and putting out a journal this winter. They hope eventually to have an office in the Black community.

All this has been accomplished since August 15th when we first opened up the office on Boylston St. The office was rented with all these things in mind. Our back room has a seating capacity of 150 people. We had the floors sanded and purchased 100 chairs. We invested in a movie projector and set up a bookstore for movement literature. Everything was geared towards building a massive and powerful Women's movement here in Boston. At the time that this statement is being run off, it is not clear whether we will be able to keep the office.

We would like to conclude this statement with a reaffirmation of our intentions to continue the struggle for this movement, which we feel is the only way to the liberation of Female human beings in this country and our sisters throughout the world.

FEMALE LIBERATION

This article takes up the place of women's liberation in the overall fight for the liberation of all humanity. Should women put aside their struggle for liberation? Why are the demands of female emancipation a threat to capitalism? It is taken here from the Female Liberation newsletter, May 2, 1971.

Why Is Feminism Revolutionary?

by Nancy Williamson
April 17, 1971

One of the questions that we're often asked is "How can you justify a demonstration around strictly feminist issues when there are so many other important issues that need attending to, i.e., war, racism, poverty, pollution?"

This is a valid question. In a country where 50 million people live in poverty, where $100 billion a year is spent on genocide, where 20 million citizens are discriminated against because of skin color, where the air we breathe, the water we drink, and the food we eat is poison, it is right to ask why do women continue to concentrate on the issues of abortion, child care, equal work for equal pay, an end to sex-role stereotyping, and an end to laws governing private sexuality.

The answer—that feminism is revolutionary and that the attainment of feminist demands would ultimately guarantee an end to the other evils that plague our society—is not self-explanatory.

On the surface, our demands do not appear revolutionary. At most we seem to be asking for things that many people think we are well on the way to attaining under the existing system.

Yet if we examine the issues more clearly, we see that in fact the five demands cannot be guaranteed under the existing system.

Free abortion on demand, free child care centers, and an end to laws governing private sexuality would guarantee women the right to control their reproductive organs and thus their entire lives. Our bodies and our lives would no longer belong to the state.

Equal work and equal pay, equal job and educational opportunity, and an end to sex-role stereotyping in jobs would guarantee each woman the right to develop herself to her fullest potential and would guarantee her a job in her chosen field. (A society that maintains unemployment at 3-1/2 billion [percent], that sees unemployment as a natural part of life, and in fact good for the economy, cannot and has no intention of giving women equal pay or the right to work. If industry paid women now employed equally to men, the payrolls would be increased by $69 billion per year.)

Capitalism cannot grant these things to women, for it is based, like all authoritarian patriarchal societies, on human oppression. The women's liberation movement, even at this moment in its embryonic stages, poses a greater threat to capitalism than any other social movement. It is impossible to liberate 53 per cent of the population without affecting complete social change. The achievement of feminist demands presupposes far-reaching changes in the sacred and seemingly immutable institutions of marriage, the family, the church, the state. Feminism challenges attitudes as well as institutions. Feminism demands that consciousness be raised while institutions are being lowered; that new systems be created while old systems are being demolished. The goals of feminism insure the liberation of all people and the creation of a life-protecting society in which human oppression will be an ugly footnote in the pages of history.

So-called revolutionaries have always admonished us to fight for socialism and thereby to end female oppression. Men in the anti-slavery movement in this country persuaded feminists to lay aside women's issues to fight for the freedom of Black people. Throughout history women have been told that our rights are not important enough to justify a separate autonomous struggle. We have listened. We have fought the struggles of every other oppressed people and have continued, as systems changed, to live in subjection. Other social movements can achieve a change in the system as they have in the past without ending female oppression as, for example, when socialist revolutions occurred in Eastern Europe without a parallel feminist revolution. Systems will change but women will not be free until women unite under the banner of feminism.

Presently a powerful dynamic women's movement is again manifesting itself around the world. And again the anti-feminist forces are deluging us with arguments aimed at undermining our confidence and persuading us to delay the struggle to fight the "larger battles." Arguments which glorify the greater importance of other causes are always aimed at destroying feminism and thus preventing the liberation of women.

The place of women at this time in history is in the feminist movement. Women's work at this time in history is advancing the feminist struggle. We will end the war, we will end capitalism and imperialism, we will end racism and guarantee people of the future an environment that is beautiful, clean, and free only if we are consistent feminists, only if we view feminism as the greater cause.

Why is feminism revolutionary: Because it will destroy the authoritarian patriarchal society which has depended for

6,000 years on the oppression of over half the human race.

Why is feminism revolutionary? Because by freeing women we free the rest of the world as well. Female oppression, the first and most universal form of human oppression, served and continues to serve as the example upon which all other forms of human oppression is based. Until women are free, the human race will wear chains.

INDEX

Page numbers in italics signify photographs or leaflets.

About Haymarket Books

Haymarket Books is a radical, independent, nonprofit book publisher based in Chicago. Our mission is to publish books that contribute to struggles for social and economic justice. We strive to make our books a vibrant and organic part of social movements and the education and development of a critical, engaged, international left.

We take inspiration and courage from our namesakes, the Haymarket martyrs, who gave their lives fighting for a better world. Their 1886 struggle for the eight-hour day—which gave us May Day, the international workers' holiday—reminds workers around the world that ordinary people can organize and struggle for their own liberation. These struggles continue today across the globe—struggles against oppression, exploitation, poverty, and war.

Since our founding in 2001, Haymarket Books has published more than five hundred titles. Radically independent, we seek to drive a wedge into the risk-averse world of corporate book publishing. Our authors include Noam Chomsky, Arundhati Roy, Rebecca Solnit, Angela Y. Davis, Howard Zinn, Amy Goodman, Wallace Shawn, Mike Davis, Winona LaDuke, Ilan Pappé, Richard Wolff, Dave Zirin, Keeanga-Yamahtta Taylor, Nick Turse, Dahr Jamail, David Barsamian, Elizabeth Laird, Amira Hass, Mark Steel, Avi Lewis, Naomi Klein, and Neil Davidson. We are also the trade publishers of the acclaimed Historical Materialism Book Series and of Dispatch Books.

Also Available from Haymarket Books

Abolition. Feminism. Now.
Angela Y. Davis, Gina Dent, Erica R. Meiners, and Beth E. Richie

Abolition Feminisms, Vol. 1:
Organizing, Survival, and Transformative Practice
Edited by Alisa Bierria, Jakeya Caruthers, and Brooke Lober
Foreword by Dean Spade

Community as Rebellion
A Syllabus for Surviving Academia as a Woman of Color
Lorgia García Peña

How We Get Free: Black Feminism and the Combahee River Collective
Edited by Keeanga-Yamahtta Taylor

Rehearsals for Living
Robyn Maynard and Leanne Betasamosake Simpson

#SayHerName
Black Women's Stories of State Violence and Public Silence
African American Policy Forum, edited by Kimberlé Crenshaw
Foreword by Janelle Monáe

We Do This 'Til We Free Us
Abolitionist Organizing and Transforming Justice
Mariame Kaba, edited by Tamara K. Nopper
Foreword by Naomi Murakawa

About the Author

Nancy Rosenstock, feminist and socialist activist for five decades, was a member of Boston Female Liberation, and served on the national staff of the Women's National Abortion Action Coalition in 1971. A member of Chicago for Abortion Rights, Rosenstock continues the fight to maintain safe, legal, and accessible abortion.